I0764158

"While the theme of this book, death and eternal life, is always relevant, it is perhaps more pertinent now than ever in the face of our current health crisis. These meditations have already consoled and strengthened the faith of many people when confronting the death or illness of someone they love. Now, by the grace of this translation, they will provide spiritual nourishment to many more."

—**CHRISTOPH SCHÖNBORN**, archbishop of Vienna

"A look which is all at once bold, candid, and full of hope into the ultimate reality which awaits each and every one of us—death. An invitation to contemplate the hour of our death in order to discover its deepest meaning. Fr. Jean-Miguel teaches us how to live while remaining mindful of death, the purpose of which is to serve as the gateway to blessed eternity."

—**KESTUTIS KEVALAS**, Archbishop of Kaunas, Lithuania

"Fr. Jean-Miguel Garrigues . . . presents the mystery of death as the culmination of our journey in this world, a loving encounter with God, who asks us to freely accept the gift of eternal life. This book encourages us to accompany the dying with compassion . . . and to prepare ourselves for the day when we, too, will be called to accomplish, in the company of Jesus, the great 'Passover' from this life to the house of our heavenly Father."

—**DOM PHILIPPE DUPONT**, Abbot of Solesmes, France

"The most human thing that Jesus did was to die. Death unites us all, even though we sometimes want to downplay or even ignore that fact. That is why this beautiful new book is for everyone. Insightful, touching, and, above all, real, *At the Hour of Our Death* is an invitation to gaze upon this quintessentially human part of our life with clear eyes, an open mind, and a trusting heart. It is an essential book about an essential part of everyone's life."

—**JAMES MARTIN**, SJ, author of *Jesus: A Pilgrimage*

At the Hour of Our Death

Saint Thérèse of Lisieux just after her death

At the Hour of Our Death

Receiving the Gift of Eternal Life

Jean-Miguel Garrigues

Translated by
Gregory Casprini

CASCADE *Books* • Eugene, Oregon

AT THE HOUR OF OUR DEATH
Receiving the Gift of Eternal Life

Cascade Books
An Imprint of Wipf and Stock Publishers
199 W. 8th Ave., Suite 3
Eugene, OR 97401

www.wipfandstock.com

PAPERBACK ISBN: 978-1-6667-1795-2
HARDCOVER ISBN: 978-1-6667-1796-9
EBOOK ISBN: 978-1-6667-1797-6

Cataloguing-in-Publication data:

Names: Garrigues, Jean-Miguel, 1944–, author. | Casprini, Gregory, translator.

Title: At the hour of our death : receiving the gift of eternal life / Jean-Miguel Garrigues ; translated by Gregory Casprini.

Description: Eugene, OR : Cascade Books, 2022 | Includes bibliographical references.

Identifiers: ISBN 978-1-6667-1795-2 (paperback) | ISBN 978-1-6667-1796-9 (hardcover) | ISBN 978-1-6667-1797-6 (ebook)

Subjects: LCSH: Death—Religious aspects—Christianity. | Church work with the terminally ill.

Classification: BV4460.6 .G37 2022 (print) | BV4460.6 .G37 (ebook)

10/14/22

To my dear friend, Cécile Reboul, with gratitude for her work in listening to and editing these conferences

We really want that which He wants, we really want, without knowing it, our troubles, our sufferings, our loneliness, even though we imagine that we only want our pleasures. We imagine ourselves fearing our death and fleeing it, when in reality we desire that death as He desired His; indeed our death is His. Just as He sacrifices himself on every altar where Mass is celebrated, He begins to die again in every man who undergoes agony. We want everything He wants, but we do not know we want it, we do not know ourselves. Sin causes us to live on the surface of ourselves, we only come into ourselves in order to die, and that is where He is waiting for us.

—GEORGES BERNANOS, *Notes*, January 1948

Contents

Translator's Foreword

Jean-Miguel Garrigues was born in 1944 in a family of Spanish diplomats at a time when his parents happened to be stationed in Istanbul (Turkey). After studying in Spain, France, and America, he entered the French province of the Dominican Order and was ordained a priest in 1969. While preparing his PhD, he spent one year, thanks to a scholarship from the World Council of Churches, at the Orthodox Faculty of Theology of Thessaloniki (Greece) and a second year at the Faculty of Theology of the Institut Catholique in Paris (ICP). In 1973 he defended a dissertation on "Divinization through Charity according to Maximus the Confessor."

Jean-Miguel Garrigues is a highly respected scholar and theologian. During the 1990s he had the honor of serving as Lenten preacher for a traditional three-year cycle at Cathedral of Notre-Dame in Paris. He collaborated on the preparation of the Catechism of the Catholic Church and helped prepare the act of repentance made by Saint John Paul II on behalf of the church in the year 2000.

Jean-Miguel is the author of twenty books on theology and spirituality as well as numerous articles. His most popular work, *God Without the Idea of Evil* (*Dieu sans idée tu mal*), which already contains many of his deepest and most original theological intuitions concerning God's merciful design of salvation, human liberty, and the problem of evil, was first published in France in 1982. An expanded edition appeared in 1990, and this was re-edited in 2016 with a preface by Cardinal Christoph Schönborn.

Father Garrigues has recently published a book along with a French Jesuit in defense of the Holy Father Pope Francis and *Amoris Laetitia*. For many years he has worked with Cardinal Schönborn in establishing contacts with Messianic Judaism. Jean-Miguel currently lives at the Dominican convent in Toulouse, where he teaches dogmatic theology. He gives numerous seminars and retreats and is often sought after as a confessor or spiritual director.

At the Hour of Our Death: Receiving the Gift of Eternal Life (*A l'heure de notre mort-Accueillir la vie éternelle*) is the fruit both of Jean-Miguel Garrigues's theological reflections and of his pastoral experience as chaplain in a hospital where he was often called upon to accompany terminally ill cancer patients. In our society today, there is a strong tendency to psychologically ignore or deny the reality of death. Many people voluntarily strive to think and live as if their existence in this world was never to end. When patients are seriously ill, their family and friends as well as the hospital personnel usually do everything they can to camouflage the possible proximity of death. At funerals, mourners and sometimes even the clergy readily evoke with nostalgia the virtues and accomplishments of the deceased but without any mention of the meaning of the act of death itself, of death as a transition or passage, the immediate and definitive access to eternal life.

Jean-Miguel Garrigues examines death in the light of Christian revelation, while drawing also on his experiences accompanying the dying. Because the human body belongs to the material world, where living things are in a state of constant change and are subject to the process of generation and corruption, death is, in a certain sense, an inevitable natural reality. It is, however, instinctively felt by almost everyone to be something extremely painful, tragic, and scandalous. Materialists, for whom man consists solely in his body, necessarily despair in the face of death, even if they strive to confront it stoically, since for them it amounts to the destruction of the human person and attests to the ultimate absurdity of man's destiny. Among those who maintain that man is composed not only of his body but also of a spiritual element, the soul, various attitudes are possible. The Eastern religions encourage people to accept death with peaceful resignation as part of the ongoing cycle of nature, with the prospect, perhaps, of spiritual liberation after a long series of reincarnations in different bodies. Certain forms of Platonistic spirituality, which have sometimes been popular even among Christians, welcome death as an immediate liberation of the soul from the prison of the body so that it can be free to enter definitively into the world of the Spirit.

Authentic Christianity, however, affirms that man was created inseparably and destined to live eternally as body and soul. Although the human body is naturally mortal, man was at the beginning created in a state of supernatural grace which would normally have prevented him from undergoing death as we experience it today, as a violent separation of the soul from its body. Instead, unfallen man, at the end of a journey on earth marked by an ever-increasing openness to and a voluntary acceptance of the inspirations of God's love, would have passed body and soul (in a manner somewhat but not entirely similar to that of the Virgin Mary in the mystery of her Assumption) into the fullness of the kingdom of heaven.

As we know, this grace that was given to humanity at the beginning was lost through the original sin of our first parents, a sin ratified later by our own personal sins. The primeval covenant that would have shielded us from death was broken and humanity has fallen back under the natural law of mortality. Therefore we must necessarily die. Our body falls into decomposition, while the soul finds itself naked before the Almighty Creator, in a state which, in addition to being a consequence of sin, is also "unnatural," since, unlike the angels who are pure spirits, our souls were meant to dwell and function in our bodies. These factors account for our metaphysical and spiritual dread in the face of death, and explain our nostalgia for the lost paradise where body and soul were destined to live eternally.

But through Jesus Christ we have been given once again the promise of eternal life and the hope of a complete restoration of our corporal and spiritual integrity. Through his death on the cross, Christ redeemed us of our sins and reconciled us with the Father. In his resurrection from the dead, we have the firstfruits of our own bodily resurrection, which will take place for the entire human race at the end of time when all creation will be transformed and the glory of the children of God manifested.

But already at the hour of our death, Jesus comes to meet each and every one of us, in order to assist our soul in its passage from this world into eternal life. He manifests to us at that time the fullness of God's love, and fights until the last instant to save us from the danger of damnation. Father Garrigues establishes an interesting link between this ultimate visitation of Christ and the mysteries of his agony at Gethsemane and his descent into hell on Holy Saturday. These two events have a dimension that in a certain sense is co-extensive to human history. Saint Catherine of Siena already saw in Christ's acceptance of the cup presented to him by the Father at Gethsemane his ardent resolution to love each one of us until the end, despite all the resistance our sins might offer to the reception of his redemptive work.

As for the Lord's descent into hell, Father Garrigues interprets it with the help of what has often appeared to be a very obscure text from the First Letter of Saint Peter, a passage where it is stated that through Christ's descent into hell, "the gospel was preached even to those who are dead" (1 Pet 4:6 ESV). According to Father Garrigues's interpretation, this means that

> in the mystery of his Passover, Christ, through his grace, meets every person in his or her death. He offers salvation even to people who refused the will of God concerning certain matters during their lives . . . [T]o every man, regardless of whether or not in his lifetime he knew Christ, regardless of whether he lived before or after Christ, regardless of whether he accepted or refused certain

> commandments of God during his lifetime, Christ offers salvation at the hour of his death. In this ultimate and mysterious meeting, the love of God is revealed to every man . . . No man is deprived of this encounter with Christ, who died for us all. If it does not happen during a person's lifetime, it at least occurs at the moment of his death . . . [W]e are not speaking here of metaphysical death, which definitively seals a person's destiny, but of the moment which precedes it and where each one must still accomplish his last act of liberty.

The hour of our death is in fact the moment when we are called upon to make our last act of liberty, an act that, as we cross the threshold of this world into the presence of God, determines our particular judgment and our destiny for all eternity. Those who, through the grace of Christ, make this passage in an act of perfect love enter directly into the light of God's presence, and this light, which is the fire of divine love, renders them eternally blessed.

Those who at the moment of death allow themselves to be loved by God, but who are as yet unable to respond by an act of perfect love because of attachments to the self and to worldly things, and who, therefore, are unable to sufficiently repair for the damage caused by their sins, enter this same divine light, which causes them to suffer in a way that purifies them and prepares them for the blessed vision of heaven. This is, in essence, purgatory—not a "temporary hell" as is sometimes falsely imagined, but a corridor leading to heaven, a state already permeated by the feeling of God's presence and where the sufferings are motivated by the impatient desire to see God face-to-face.

As for those who at the moment of death choose to definitively reject divine grace, hardening themselves in an act of egoism and pride, they too enter into the light of God's presence. But the eternal flame of God's love, which renders blessed the saints of heaven and purifies the souls of purgatory, is experienced by them as the source of unending torment. Such is in essence the damnation of hell.

Alongside these rich doctrinal considerations, our author gives us a set of interesting observations drawn from the experiences he himself or others have made in accompanying the dying. Those who during their lives have earnestly sought to receive and model themselves according to Christ's self-sacrificing "love unto folly," a love that enables man to love God perfectly above all things and his neighbor *more* (in a certain sense) than himself, tend to surrender themselves gently and easily to the Lord when he comes to meet them at the moment of death. They seem to plunge into eternal life like ripe fruit falling off a tree.

In his work as hospital chaplain, Father Garrigues observed an interesting evolution in patients who had become seriously ill at a period when they still were busily immersed in worldly affairs, giving little thought to God or eternity. At first, many of these patients seemed to be in revolt against their situation, angry, impatient, aggressive, full of despair, with a tendency to bitterly accuse others, themselves, or God for their misfortune. But as time went on, with the approach of death, these same people became serene, grateful, loving, and forgiving. At the moment of death they seemed prepared to give themselves up gently into the hands of God. It should be noted that this "conversion to love" took place not only among persons with a religious background, and regardless of whether or not they had been practicing their faith, but also among unbelievers. The latter were almost never able to express their conversion of heart in religious terms, but they manifested it in a real way by the most simple and even banal words or gestures.

On the other hand, our author notes that in some rare instances there are people who, at the approach of death, seem to harden into a state of anger and unforgiveness. Despite physical extenuation, they are as if unable to die, and their agony seems to go on indefinitely. Their death becomes a terrible struggle precisely because God wants to save them and does not want to take them in the hardened state into which they are closing themselves. Such is the mystery of the last moments of life. Those who have been revived from deep comas after having been pronounced clinically dead, as well as those who have survived after almost perishing in a car accident or through drowning, often attest that when a person comes close to this ultimate frontier of earthly existence, he is able to suddenly recall in a flash all the moments of his life while at the same time feeling torn between the attraction to the light of love and an opposite temptation to choose the self instead, to close himself up in the darkness of pride. And thus, although there exists at that moment a real risk of incurring eternal damnation, the grace of the Lord who wants us all to be saved is vehemently at work until the last instant, and this action can only be thwarted by the most resolute refusal of human liberty. Therefore, while it is necessary to fear damnation, it is possible to hope and pray that no member of the human race ever has or ever will be eternally condemned alongside Satan and his fallen angels, but will enter instead, perhaps after going through a stage of purification in purgatory, into the blessed vision of God in the company of the angels and saints.

Jean-Miguel Garrigues's *At the Hour of Our Death* is a book that nourishes the vitally important theological virtue of hope. It encourages us to accompany the dying with compassion, love, and prayer, to live in communion with the saints of heaven and the holy souls of purgatory, and also to wisely and serenely prepare ourselves for the day when we too will be called to accomplish, in the company of Jesus, the great Passover from this life to the house of our heavenly Father. Father Garrigues introduces us into the contemplation of the communion of saints, the mystery celebrated each year by the church on All Saints Day and All Souls' Day. His book is an exhortation to "desire," in the words of Saint Benedict, "eternal life with a most ardent spiritual longing,"[1] to aspire for the day when we shall take our place in the kingdom of heaven, where, together with all the children of God, we will improvise an unending song of love, a symphony of praise in honor of the Blessed Trinity.

Gregory Casprini, OSB
Monk of Saint Benedict's Monastery, Palendriai
July 11, 2019, Feast of Saint Benedict

1. In the original French edition, Jean-Miguel Garrigues quotes authors without providing precise reference indications. In the present English version, these quotations are my own translations of the original.

Preface

THIS BOOK IS A collection of lectures given to parishioners at the Church of Saint-Nizier in Lyons. Although the text has been revised, I have voluntarily sought to preserve its character as a talk directly addressed to listeners. Readers can well understand how difficult it would be to treat a subject like this one without getting personally involved.

My view of death comes from my experience as a priest serving in parishes and in a hospital chaplaincy. My approach is therefore all at once theological, pastoral, and spiritual. This presupposes a philosophical look at death as a human experience, which can be found among other places in a book by P. Marie-Dominique Goutierre, FJ, entitled *L'homme face à sa mort: l'absurde ou le salut?* (*Man Facing His Death: The Absurd or Salvation?*), published in French by Parole et Silence.

Acknowledgments

THIS ENGLISH TRANSLATION WAS done in close collaboration with the author, Jean-Miguel Garrigues. We would both like to specially thank Michael Centore who carefully edited and formatted the manuscript, as well as Elena Leontjeva for her suggestions and encouragement, and Br. Gérard Landron for his technical assistance.

1

Faith in the Face of Our Condition as Mortals

Dare We Speak of Death from the Vantage Point of the Faith?

DEATH CONCERNS US ALL: we are all mortal, we are all confronted with the mystery of our own death and the death of others, and we can never really separate these two aspects. Paradoxically, no one, or hardly any one, speaks about death any more from an authentically Christian viewpoint. Even in funeral sermons, priests tend to eulogize the past life of the deceased person in an almost pagan manner while avoiding placing the assembly in front of the mystery of death.

One of the great shortcomings of present-day catechesis, understood in the broadest sense as the preaching of the church, is the failure to confront the mystery of death head on. This evasion is a relatively recent phenomenon. The *Spiritual Exercises* of Saint Ignatius of Loyola, which for centuries helped to form the spiritual life of a great many Catholics, begins by asking the believers to meditate on death and by inviting them to contemplate the mystery of their own death. This sometimes led to certain excesses. It is said that in one house where the spiritual exercises were given, the retreat began in front of a catafalque draped in black! This evokes a vision of death bequeathed to us by the nineteenth century, with black catafalques, horses draped in black, hearses, black shrouds adorned with tears, and silver bones: a vision full of pathos but having very little to do with Christianity.

It is difficult to find the right words when talking about death, and although our faith provides us with much enlightenment, we continue to stand before the mystery of death as if we were confronting an enigma. I have been surprised sometimes when talking with those who have recently lost someone dear to them, to find that even very genuine believers can react to death almost like pagans. All of a sudden one encounters a kind of skepticism, as if faith had nothing to teach us concerning death, and therefore about the afterlife—since for believers, death is the passage into the afterlife. I have been appalled to see how, around a person who is dying, fervent believers sometimes react with panic in a totally pagan manner, as if suddenly, in the face of death, their faith has been put on hold.

Christians today do not speak of death anymore; at best they speak of the resurrection as a very distant reality. Otherwise they talk about sickness, decrepitude, or the fact that someone is coming to the "end of his days." But one hardly ever hears people speaking anymore about the act of death itself, of death as a transition, as a passage, an access.

It is with the eyes of faith that I will try to consider here the mystery of death, seeing it as an access to eternal life but also as our way of receiving eternal life. We often think of death as an enigmatic passage, beyond which, we are willing to hope, eternal life is found. I, on the contrary, would like to maintain that death itself, considered in various ways, is the reception of eternal life.

There is not death and then eternal life. Death itself is an anticipation, a beginning, and therefore a welcoming of eternal life. I am fond of these words of Saint Teresa of Ávila: "We do not die of death, we die of life"; that is to say, we die because eternal life bursts in upon us, and at the same time puts an end to our mortal existence. This may seem like a scandalous paradox to many, because what we see first in a being who is dying is the end of his earthly existence. We are witnessing the end or conclusion of a certain regime or mode of life. But in this conclusion, the eyes of faith can already discern the presence of eternal life—not on the other side, but on this side of death. In fact, our life itself leads us to death because our mortal life is made to welcome eternal life. Our life in this world is already drawn towards eternal life, and this intimate inclination finally increases to the breaking point when our temporal life falls into eternal life.

Listening to Saint Thérèse, the "Little Flower"

In this meditation we will seek the help of Saint Thérèse of Lisieux, the "little flower," who can perhaps be considered the great patron saint of death for our time. She died young, after a very long agony. For months she could see death coming. She left us a notebook containing her last words, now published under the title *Entering into Life*.

Two short sayings will guide this meditation. When Thérèse was asked, "What will you die from?" She answered: "I will die of death." At first glance this seems to be a tautology, a truism. But it really takes a great deal of faith to speak in this way. True, we are led to death's door by many things—illnesses, accidents—and we are driven to death by various factors, but in the final analysis, we die only from death. Death is an inexplicable mystery that cannot be reduced to mere physical degradation, and that cannot be identified with the various elements that precede and prepare it.

Another saying of Saint Thérèse of Lisieux illuminates this first affirmation: "I am not dying, I am entering life." This phrase apparently contradicts the previous statement. But Thérèse maintains that our death itself is already an entrance into eternal life and that such is, in fact, the mystery of death. This mystery implies that we are invaded by eternal life. Such is the life that Thérèse has in mind when she says, "I am entering into life."

Death always implies a mystery of freedom: God's freedom in coming to us, but also our freedom in welcoming God. Death is an encounter between two persons who are free. As soon as we grasp this fact, we are liberated from a fatalistic, pagan fear of death. It is quite normal for us to be fearful of the sufferings, the illnesses, or the accidents that prepare death. But when we understand that the hour of our death is an encounter—I would even go so far as to say an encounter of love between God and us—we open our hearts to the true mystery of death. Our death is a free decision on the part of God, even if the Lord makes use of secondary causes so that, from a human point of view, it is a combination of circumstances that brings us, through an illness or an accident, to the end of our bodily life. In reality, God governs these secondary causes without falsifying them. He knows them in the eternal present of his transcendence and they are in his hands. The design of love that he has for us, the word of love that he has for us, passes through these secondary causes in such a way that even through our illness, even through our agony, the moment of death remains the mystery of a free divine decision and a free human response.

Hence we can see how totally anti-Christian it is to engage in any prognosis on death. Even from a medical point of view, assessing the amount of time a person has left to live is something very precarious. Serious physicians refrain from doing this, except maybe in private among themselves, as a pure clinical hypothesis. Such a prognosis must absolutely not be revealed to the patient, even if he asks for it, not only out of delicacy for his feelings, but simply because in all likelihood the subsequent course of events will probably render it invalid. The complexity of the human organism is such, and its connection to the soul so deep, that it is absolutely impossible to predict the moment of death. In the eyes of faith, this unpredictable nature of death stems from the fact that it is a mystery of God's freedom and love for us. It is He who sets the time of the definitive encounter. As Saint John of the Cross said, "Lord, tear away this thin veil that still separates us." During his mystical encounters with the Lord, Saint John of the Cross yearned for death in order to enter into the vision of God "face-to-face."

Death: A Loving Encounter between Two Liberties

Death is also a free response on the part of man. Those of us who have accompanied the dying know how totally disconcerted we can feel when we realize that the patient, mysteriously, is free in the face of death. Of course one dies due to an illness or an accident, but in a more ultimate way one dies when one agrees to die. There is a mystery of acquiescence, a last act of liberty on the part of the man who answers the call of God and comes to meet him. Some patients, by refusing to die, succeed in prolonging endlessly their agony. This happens simply because they are not ready; they are afraid of the final encounter. The preparation for death is closely linked to the preparation of our liberty and of our soul for the encounter with God. The free and mysterious character of the moment of our death makes it impossible for us to look upon it as an end inevitably programmed by one or another disease that we may in fact, or at least potentially, be carrying within ourselves. This is the moment God has chosen to tell us, "Come," and when we answer, "Yes, Lord, I am coming."

We no longer dare speak of death, because in the Christian discourses on faith we do not dare speak sufficiently about the intimacy of the personal encounter between each of us and God. On the other hand, the mystics readily speak about death, because their experience of heart-to-heart encounters with God during prayer prepares them for this final yes, to the point that they actually desire it. Having witnessed the death of several contemplative nuns, I have been very much struck to see how easily they die. Their agony can be very painful, but that's another question. I speak of death itself. The chaplain of a contemplative monastery once said to me, "They die like ripe fruits falling to the ground; the Lord picks them up like fruit that is ready to come off the tree. They die very simply." Indeed, in the context of the monastic life, death seems to be exorcised. Witnessing the agony of a contemplative nun, the burial of a Carthusian monk in a tomb that does not even bear his name, or that of a Trappist, straight into the ground, wrapped in his cowl, helps one to grasp the very natural side of death, death accepted with a kind of simplicity and even joy, not out of contempt for earthly life, but because this entire earthly life has been a preparation for the ultimate encounter of love with the Lord.

Running Away from Death

It is painful to note nowadays the extent to which death, even among families who believe in God, has in practice been deprived of its Christian signification. In the past, when I was called to pray over someone who had just died, I often sensed a great deal of uneasiness among the people who invited me to do so; some would hardly even dare enter the departed person's room, and there was even one family who, when I arrived, just continued watching television in the living room while saying to me, "Oh yes, Grandma is in her room at the end of the hall, please go and pray over her there!"

The loss of a relationship with God results in the impossibility of facing death, our own or that of others. I don't deny that there is in sickness and suffering something very hard to look at. But I am speaking here of the fear of being in the presence of a corpse, of this almost superstitious attitude in the presence of a dead person. We have become incapable of perceiving a reality that is full of humble simplicity. I have always been struck by the humility of the dead. The trace of eternal life in the mortal remains that have become so humble indicates a kind of birth. Death has the same humility as a birth: someone who dies is very small, like someone who is born. But precisely during the intermediate parentheses that we call life, earthly life, people seek to be great, to make and shape themselves, to build themselves up. They do not want to look upon their smallness, and thus they are unable to confront death.

This running away from death concerns not only families, but also doctors and nurses in hospitals. Having been, for a time, the chaplain of a cancer treatment center, I remember these words spoken to me by a dying person: "The doctor does not come anymore, even the nurses hardly come anymore, why? They are afraid, they are afraid of me, they know that I am going to die, they are running away!" There would be much to say about a certain attitude towards death that is commonly found in the medical profession. Death contradicts an entire dream concerning the omnipotence of modern medicine, as if medicine were intended to render man immortal.

Some doctors look upon death as a terrible failure and cannot accept it. This can lead them to ethical behaviors that seem to oppose each other (though the opposites are in the same category), ranging from therapeutic obstinacy to euthanasia. This pair of opposites expresses the same refusal of the mystery of death. Therapeutic obstinacy is pursued until the moment when nothing further can be done; at that moment the decision is made to suppress the human life. This deeply pagan attitude is, unfortunately, very widespread. It is not a question of challenging the very real technical value of medicine and doctors, but of noting that many cannot accept death. They believe that their purpose is to cure, as if they were going to make man immortal. But the goal of the doctor is to give care, which is somewhat different. Care, of course, aims at healing, but healing itself is a mystery, like life, like death.

I am fond of recalling the beautiful phrase of Ambroise Paré, a great Protestant surgeon of the sixteenth century, who said concerning his patients, "I give them care, but it is God who heals them." To give care involves doing all that is possible to help foster human life. But as for life itself, the doctor does not give it, it is not in his hands. It is in his power neither to give it nor to remove it. The dream of medical omnipotence, expressed by therapeutic obstinacy, can ultimately result in the dreadful decision to destroy a patient's life when it becomes clear that he or she can no longer be cured.

Accepting Ourselves as Mortals

We can say with Saint Augustine: "As soon as we are born, we begin to die." At the same time, and for precisely the very same reason, we can say that we enter, through the grace of the Christ's Passover, into eternal life.

But do we really start to die from the moment of birth? Well, apparently not. And nonetheless, even if for twenty, twenty-five, thirty years, our being is in a state of biological growth and development, the forces of deterioration are also already at work. This paradox is found especially in our nervous system: the nerve cells do not multiply, and our mental development progresses only because we use more and more efficiently a nervous system that is in fact gradually dying. We put it to better and better use, until a moment when it gives way because it has become all bungled up. It is curious to note that this growth of our most elevated bodily faculty takes place on the basis of an underlying death. On the other hand, we constantly carry within us quantities of viruses and microbes, which can at any time endanger our lives. This is the case even for small children. There are, alas, little children who die, as, for example, when a nursling dies suddenly in a senselessly unpredictable way, or when children perish due to an infection or a malformation that is impossible to correct.

And thus no one is safe from death. We are all born mortal, we are born already marked by death, and it is only by trying to forget this reality that we can delude ourselves into believing that our present life is immortal. This is exactly what many of our contemporaries, even Christians, try to do, living as though death does not concern them, as if death were only the death of others. And even then, are we really able to confront the death of others? Is it not true that we seek above all to close our eyes so as not to see it?

When Saint Augustine says, "As soon we are born we begin to die, in beginning to live, we begin to die," he states a fundamental truth. Our life is going to develop but always on a certain foundation of mortality. Life and entropy coupled together are already visible on the cosmic plane: we can note a growing organization of matter even up through living things, but this organization is then coupled with a loss of energy that digs a sort of hole from below, involving the cycle of generation and corruption. We, too, in our own lives, tend to wear ourselves out: the way we live sometimes prepares our death. For example, if we eat too well, we risk contracting cardiovascular diseases and thus we actually "dig our grave with our teeth." Indeed, death is not only prepared by life's disorders, but also, more simply, by its very intensity. When we live more intensely, burning more energy, we can in a certain sense hasten the moment of our death. We must therefore accept this fundamental reality that we are not born immortal. We need to give up the dream of a terrestrial immortality. It is not a matter of renouncing the desire for immortality that we carry deep within us, but of renouncing the illusion of wanting to fulfill that desire in this life.

Our Future Does Not Belong to Us

We live, we speak, and around us life and the world go on, as if no one was ever going to die. Everyone of course knows that he is going to die someday, but everyone acts as if this were not the case. As a result, we seek continually to program the future. Among the customs of the church I very much appreciate the fact that, at least up until quite recently, no official text ever spoke of the future—or, when it had to do so in order to announce the date of some convocation, for example, the Magisterium always used the formula *Deo volente*, that is to say, "God willing." I am always a little surprised when I hear a certain way of talking about the future, even from pastors of the church. I can't help but say to myself, "After all, how do we as Christians (or as Jews, since we share with them the same hope) know if there still *will be* time?" We cannot really talk with any certainty about the future. Aristotle stated that there is no science about future events, contingent future events, which may or may not occur. We can make predictions, but these predictions are not certified truths, they are only conjectures. By definition, the future is not an object of science, because science concerns that which always and necessarily occurs, whereas the future is only a possibility, and therefore remains in its enigmatic contingency, as long as it has not been fulfilled in the present.

Moreover, in the Bible, Christ tells us, "It is not for you to know the times or the seasons that the Father has fixed by his own authority" (Acts 1:7 ESV). Whenever a society like our own projects itself into the future with a claim of certainty, it does so through a certain negation of God. Now it is normal that there be a consideration of future prospects, but while these can only be, at very best, probable hypotheses, they quickly take on the aspect of proven certainties in the eyes of people, who will later be obliged to revise their prospects! It is an extraordinary experience to read old newspapers. What is written there has nothing to do with history, because history is written afterwards. With hindsight, the events seem very coherent. But when one looks back at what the press wrote at the time the events were taking place, one realizes that it is something quite different from history as it was told later. Examples like these invariably show how people enter the future blindfolded, with their heads full of misconceptions. For example, it is amusing to see how in 1900 people conceived what life would be like in the year 2000. Sometimes there is this or that element that has been verified, but, on so many other points, those who claimed to foresee the future were completely wrong. Why? Precisely because they thought they could shape the future by starting from the present, which they imagined they knew perfectly well. A will to shape the future is a will to put death in brackets. On the other hand, to live in the face of death is to accept the fact that we do not hold the future in our hands.

While accompanying cancer patients, I was able to grasp how much wisdom is achieved by people who are, as they say, "condemned" (that is, who are in the same situation as the rest of humanity, since we are all condemned to death with a delay, the only difference being that these patients have become more aware of how short that delay can be). These people have learned to live from day to day, that is to say, in the present moment, in all its intensity, without projecting themselves into the future. As for us, we project ourselves continually into the future because we forget about death and seek to put it in parentheses. We live in the future, which means that we no longer live in the present moment; we are so involved in anticipating the future that the present escapes us.

Give Up Trying to Control Time

The wisdom that places us face-to-face with death teaches us to accept renouncing our efforts to exercise control over time: control over the future, obviously, but also, in a certain sense, over the past. I believe that death purifies us even in relation to the past, the past that we somehow try to store up in ourselves. Of course, we do need to keep past events in our hearts, on condition that we do so in order to give thanks to God. We must commemorate the past, as the entire Bible invites us to do: the psalms and all the prayers of Israel are in fact a memorial. But to commemorate the past is quite the opposite of a certain type of nostalgia that binds us to the past. Instead it is an offering of love, a celebration. We are called to turn our past into a liturgy, and besides, in heaven we will celebrate the liturgy of our own past together with that of the entire family of redeemed humanity.

But there is more. I love a phrase of Jacques Maritain where he says that in heaven "the angels will tell us their history." The history of the cosmos and especially the history of humanity: the history of human freedom is something so complex, so rich, that even in the entire communion of the saints in heaven, when all men, having become transparent to one another in the love of God, will be able reveal themselves to one another while somehow offering up to God the great liturgy of history, the "input" of the angelic world will still be necessary. There are things that the angels alone have seen and that only they can tell us. First, about all that precedes human history, the entire history of the pre-human cosmos, of the immense extra-human cosmos. The cosmos has been entrusted to the care of the angels, and it is they who will enable us to understand it. It is impossible to understand the cosmos if we refuse references to the invisible world. And it is the angels who will give us knowledge of that world. Thus, in heaven we will offer to the Lord the liturgy of the bygone world, not as a song of nostalgia, as the expression of a desire to turn back, but as a great feast of thanksgiving, a memorial that renders everything present through the giving of thanks. We are in fact called to start doing this here and now. And just as we must already learn to live according to a certain "duty of improvidence" (Jacques Rivière)—a certain form of abandonment to divine providence by accepting our death and accepting that the future does not belong to us—so too must we accept a certain dispossession with regard to the past.

In this regard, I fully appreciate the extraordinary wisdom of the principles of the consecrated religious life under which I live, principles that oblige the brothers to keep practically nothing, not only to have no personal property, but also to detach themselves from vestiges of the past. During my seven years of formation we had to change the "cell" in which we lived every six months. As a result, we were strongly encouraged not to keep too many archives, letters, photos . . . I have always felt a certain discomfort with the desire to freeze time. There is nothing more melancholy than an old photograph except, as I said, in the context of celebration of the God who is eternal and who always remains in the present. Outside of that context, photographs often tend to be quite dreary, because they show above all the "irreparable outrages inflicted by time," as Racine said. They force us to contemplate our mortality and see it with a look of nostalgia, that is to say, in a very pagan way, as if time were irretrievably "lost."

If we in the religious life are called to divest ourselves as much as possible from the traces of the past, it is so that we can perceive that this past is in fact truly present in us because it has shaped us. It has shaped us for eternity. This is the way in which the past remains present; not as something bygone, but as a part of my "today." If I am what I am today, it is because I was this child, this teenager, this young man who walked along these particular paths and not along others. If, on the contrary, I insist on striving to retrieve my past as such, I risk getting caught up in the desperate and haunting spiral of "the search for lost time." We cannot retrieve lost time, even if it happens that our memory brings us back to a past event in a kind of flash through this or that perception or photo. But such an experience can contaminate our memory, creating a kind of poison which that to an illusory denial of death. In actual fact, my past continues to exist within me and it is also in front of me. Is my past anything other than the people I have encountered? And are not these my companions for all eternity? Even if I have lost sight of them now, I will find them in God. Thus they do not belong to the past. What belongs to the past are the stages of a life that passes on, and which must be accepted as such. We must not try to congeal the past or attempt to relive it in our imagination. It is just as unhealthy to relive one's past in nostalgia as it is to refuse to grow old. There is as much paganism here as in the manipulation of the future in the hope of bolstering one's sense of security.

We engage quite spontaneously in types of behavior such as these, and this shows that the spirit of the gospel has not yet penetrated deeply enough within us. When I need to get rid of old letters from friends who still remain very dear to me, because they belong to the past stages of my life, I can only resolve to do so by praying, "My Lord and God, I know that doing this will set me free! These people live on; even those who have died are with you and therefore they are more alive than me! Let us place the past into your hands; we will discover it again with you, in your eternal present, and there we will celebrate it." It is fine to recall someone again and to evoke this or that moment of the past in order to give thanks, because in that way one enters into God's present moment. But if, on the contrary, we recall things only to feel the voluptuous but completely poisonous morbidity of nostalgia, then it is something harmful that gnaws at the soul. Nostalgia for the past and programming for the future, each in its own way, steal from our soul the present, and the present is God. Indeed, God dwells in the present and only in the present. By losing the present, we lose God, and we are no longer in the place where our life is really playing out.

Free to See God Face-to-Face

Death sets us free, free for that which is the very goal of our lives: to see God. In order to remind us of this truth in our time, God chose a poor fellow sentenced to death for a sordid crime involving robbery and murder. Jacques Fesch was guillotined in France during the 1950s. He was a young man, not yet thirty years old. His life until his arrest was that of a miserably insignificant petty thief, a quite uninteresting person at first sight. After being tried and sentenced to death, he was held alive for a number of months before his execution. But during the time he spent in prison, he went through an absolutely amazing spiritual journey in connection with the well-known stigmatized French mystic Marthe Robin. At the time, not much was said about her involvement because she wanted it to be kept a secret. But Marthe was in epistolary contact with several prisoners sentenced to death. She managed to send each of them a letter and offered to correspond with them during the time preceding their execution. In this way Fesch, assisted by Robin's prayers and intercession, and also by the chaplain of the prison, went through an astonishing path of conversion.

This story shows us that in reality every human being is interesting. Jacques Fesch has left us his correspondence, notes written in prison going right up to the very night of his execution. One of the last sentences he wrote in his notebook was: "*In five hours, I will see Jesus.*" It is under this title that his writings have been published. I believe that there is no stronger statement in the face of death; it is like an echo of the little Thérèse: "I am entering into life." To certain people God gives exceptional graces in order to enlighten our faith, and so as not to leave us in the dark.

The face-to-face encounter with death puts us before the presence of God, which is a presence of love. It is this presence alone that fills our entire life and gives it its true meaning. During the months that separated him from his execution, Jacques Fesch lived each day with maximum intensity. Because he was fully alive, he had already triumphed over death. Whereas when we flee death, seeking to forget our mortality through what Pascal refers to as "distractions," these only have the effect of causing us to run ahead even faster into death's arms. No one is more marked by death than people who frantically seek to deny it. Their being is already eaten away by it, in their excessive quest for things like pleasure, power, or knowledge. Indeed, they are in the process of denying the most basic truth of their lives; they are refusing "the moment of truth."

The Moment of Truth

It would be impossible here not to mention Georges Bernanos, who was perhaps the greatest revealer of the mystery of death in literature. All his works revolve around the mystery of death, the fundamental mystery in which man's destiny, his spiritual destiny, is played out. Bernanos himself lived his death intensely. The saints in his novels die in a lucid and sometimes dramatic way, whereas the reprobates, or at least those who appear to be such (without presuming to judge the secret of their soul) "do not see themselves dying." We often hear people say, "How lucky that person was: he did not see himself die!" Bernanos, on the contrary, presents this as a sign of condemnation: it is not good to desire such a death. On the contrary, he who responds to the grace of God sees himself dying and accepts to die.

The testimony of Saint Thérèse of the Child Jesus, that of Jacques Fesch, or Franck, a young AIDS patient who died several years ago and whom Father Daniel-Ange accompanied during the last stage of his life, show us how much we must live without turning a blind eye to reality, to that which is, in a certain sense, the imminence of our own death. The privileged people mentioned above give us an increased awareness of the way in which we should constantly live. Of course, we cannot constantly live this reality as intensely as they did, but they show us the true meaning of our lives. Many false values, many false priorities would vanish if we were obliged to confront the reality of our death.

This is why the reference to our last hour is placed at the beginning of the *Spiritual Exercises* of Saint Ignatius of Loyola. The mysticism of Saint Ignatius is very much oriented towards the practical life, towards action. In the *Exercises*, it is therefore a question of seeing clearly what one has to do with one's life in relation to God. So we are put in front of our own death, precisely in order to take charge of our lives head on, establishing a correct hierarchy of urgencies and priorities. If we knew we only had a few weeks or months to live, would we necessarily make the same choices we are making now? True, we do not know how much time we have left, but at least we know that we will one day die and that our death could occur at any moment. This should situate us in a light of truth that enables us to authentically see and judge the value of what we are doing or not doing, what we are taking and what we are leaving.

The saints bear witness to this truth, and so, in its own way, does the monastic life in the church. Why does the church invite people to adopt this program of dispossession? Because it allows one to be free for the presence of God. Why are we called to give up a certain number of things? Because, whatever happens, we will not be able to take them with us to the grave. As Job declares: "Naked I came out from my mother's womb, and naked shall I return" (Job 1:21 ESV). There is therefore no point in storing things up. Would we want to die like the pharaohs, mummified, surrounded by our domestic animals, themselves mummified, our objects, our utensils? Do we want to turn our death into something like a Pharaoh's pyramid? That is the question. Do we imagine that we will be carrying something away with us, or do we accept the fact that by definition, we are merely sojourners, "strangers and pilgrims on the earth" (Heb 11:13 KJV)? It is only by accepting this fact that we really become ourselves. Because we are not simply beings who are passing away into the insignificant, into the ephemeral, into that which is degraded and lost; we are passing into God. But "God is love" (1 John 4:16 ESV), and "love never ends" (1 Cor 13:8 ESV). In him nothing is lost, even that which is taken away from us, even what life in this world inexorably tears away from us.

As an icon to keep in view during the reading of these meditations on death, I would suggest the photo of Saint Thérèse of Lisieux taken just after she died.[1] This photo is like a visible manifestation of eternal life on the face of a woman deceased. Little Thérèse has never seemed more alive in any of her other photos, where she sometimes appears a bit stilted, slightly absentminded;

1. We know that this photo has been retouched and that the original plate has disappeared. But, according to Father François de Sainte Marie (who assigns to this snapshot the number 46 in his work on the iconography relating to Saint Thérèse of Lisieux), the retouching is of little significance. We can therefore rely on this document.

she has never been more deeply concentrated on life than through her closed eyes, her smile, and the light that radiates from her entire face. She has truly "entered into life."

2

Why Does Man Rebel Against His Mortal Condition?

Death Is Something Both Natural and Scandalous

WHY IS IT THAT, here and now, we are mortal? The answers given by believers to this question often go from one extreme to the other. First of all, it is said that human nature is mortal because it has, as a substantial conditioning, an animal body, and that, like all animal and bodily natures, it is subject to generation and corruption. We are therefore mortal by nature. This is true. There is in death a natural aspect that is, actually, very consoling from a certain point of view. It was only after accompanying someone right up to death's door, holding him in my arms as he breathed his last breath, that I was able to realize that death has this natural side.

It is important to open oneself to this aspect because this is the way a large portion of humanity still perceives death today. We Christians are tempted to say that such an attitude is fatalism. But it's not all that simple. I still recall being deeply impressed and moved by images of the Vietnam War, showing all the simplicity, dignity, and humility with which the Asian population suffered so many calamities and death itself. Let's not say too quickly that this is just Asian resignation, Oriental fatalism. There is certainly some truth in this behavior. I don't say it's the entire truth, far from it, but certainly a part of the truth that constitutes a great lesson for us Westerners who are so afraid of death. An entire portion of humanity is not afraid of death and welcomes it with a kind of simplicity, like a natural event, which is part of the cycle of the cosmos and of our own nature. There is a natural dimension here: because our being is bodily, our person is destined to know death.

But having said this, I immediately sense all the dignity of the man who revolts and says, "No, I am not made for death. It's not my destiny." Obviously the Christian faith, together with an entire part of the Old Testament, but also of Greek philosophy, goes powerfully in this direction. We are made for life, for eternal life. "I have no pleasure in the death of the wicked," says God, "but that the wicked turn from his way and live" (Ezek 33:11 ESV). And while the Christian does perceive death as natural, he at the same time senses it to be a calamity, something that is unacceptable, revolting, and scandalizing. The biblical tradition gradually deepened this perception: death is something accidental, something that ought not to happen. "It's not possible, no, it should not have happened." How many times have we not heard words of this kind, or have we not uttered them ourselves, when someone has died?

These two spontaneous attitudes correspond to two explanations of death that express two complementary truths. The first perceives our bodily being as mortal, as destined first to grow and then to decline. Just as we are born, going through the process of generation, so too must we go through corruption, decomposition, decay. The entire visible cosmos lives according to this rhythm of generation and corruption. Why should we escape it, since we too are bodily in nature like the rest of the cosmos? Is not the bodily dimension, which we have in common with animals, also part of our destiny?

Death Remains Dramatic

How is it then that we still sense death to be an inadmissible contradiction? It is because we at the same time perceive that our soul is immortal. We do not accept that our destiny is linked to the corruptibility of our body. We find this repugnant because there is in our personal being a paradoxical conjunction of a bodily principle and a spiritual principle, which is the soul. Our soul declares to us constantly, "Yes, you are your body, but your body exists through me. It is by me, who am immortal, that your mortal body exists. Therefore, the mortal destiny of your body is not your ultimate destiny." This awareness can bring a kind of peace, as we see among the ancient Greeks. Let us take, for example, the story of Socrates's death. His death is tragic because he is forced to commit suicide by order of the state. But he finishes his life peacefully, explaining to his disciples that, through the immortality of his soul, he is now going to attain the true life that is spiritual. Released, as it were, from this tomb that is the body, his soul will be able to fly to the realm of ideas and the pure spirit.

Why in this context does death no longer seem to be tragic? In Greece, the Platonic tradition perceived it as a liberation, and one finds an analogous attitude, under a different form, in the Asian religions, be it Buddhism or Hinduism: death is seen as a liberation from the enslavement of the body and from its transitory, perishable nature. And yet in the West the biblical tradition is so well ingrained in us that we continue to find death repugnant. We refuse to accept it either as a simple natural fact, or even as the liberation of the soul.

It is true that during the nineteenth century, even in Christian circles, there was a certain presentation of death imbued with peaceful serenity. Gabriel Fauré's *Requiem* offers a striking artistic expression to this attitude. The soul escapes from the mortal body like a bird that takes flight and ascends into the spiritual realm. This was actually a pseudo-Christian Platonism, mixed with romanticism, which considered man to be a sort of fallen angel in the body. Death, freeing the angel from his corporeality, allowed him to fly back to heaven. This presentation was not authentically Christian, and it does not have much to say to the sensitivities of people in our time. Today, in the face of death, we meet either an attitude of faith or else a reaction of irrational, desperate revolt. We find this second attitude particularly in the existentialist current: death is absurd, repugnant, but it must be confronted stoically because it is inevitable. The only possible attitude is to face up serenely, as far as possible, to that which is absurd.

There is therefore an irrational revolt against death, and if today in hospitals even people who claim to be materialists are so traumatized by it, if doctors and nurses often flee the dying without daring to speak to them or accompany them to the end, this is because everyone experiences a terrible anguish in the face of death. Underlying this revolt, however, great perceptions can be found: not only that of the immortality of the soul, but something more, an aspiration towards the eternal life of the body itself. As caricatural as it may be, today's therapeutic obstinacy, which is often very agnostic in nature, reflects a deep perception. Not only do we yearn for spiritual survival, but more obscurely, for the eternal life of the body. We cannot seem to resign ourselves to the death of our body; we can accept it neither as a mere cosmic fatality that is part of the lot of all creatures nor as a liberation of the spiritual element in us.

It is very interesting to try to understand the sensitivity of our Western tradition, even in its caricatures, because it was molded by the biblical revelation. Why do we aspire to eternal life in our body and not only in our souls? Why do we not simply content ourselves with the immortality of the soul, or, if we are materialists, why can't we resign ourselves to the inevitability of our return to nothingness? Why does this return to nothingness cause us so much anxiety? This is obviously because the immortality of the soul in us protests against this idea. We have the perception of something in us that is immortal. The return to nothingness of the body makes us extremely anxious because we do not know how our immortal spiritual principle, which is the soul, can subsist otherwise than by being incarnate in a body. We have no experience of what it is like to be a soul separated from the body. This provokes in us a great anxiety, not only because we have not yet experienced this state, but also and above all because it is something quite violent and unnatural for a human being to live as a soul deprived of its body. Unlike the angels, who were created by God as pure spirits, we are created as incarnate spirits. Losing our body injures the integrity of our person. The idea is therefore difficult for us to bear.

Death Damages the Integrity of Our Human Person

The body is part of the human person. To lose one's body is to be damaged in one's personal integrity. Saint Thomas Aquinas goes so far as to say that in the hereafter, before the resurrection of the dead, even the saints reigning with God in heaven but who are still without their bodies continue to be deprived of their integrity. We are extremely anxious because we cannot experience death as a liberation of the soul. The body is not a mere capsule, a receptacle, a vehicle, a mechanism, an instrument at the service of the soul. It is the material organism that receives from the soul its form and its life. We *are* therefore our body. Our soul gives form to the body, that is, its being, structure, life, growth, and organization. But we do not know how the soul can exist without the body. The only real answer is God himself. In fact, the soul depends more on God, its Creator, than on its body. This is the only way to explain the current situation of the dead. When we leave our body, we are immersed in the eternity of God, and this is how our soul will exist even without its body. But we will be nonetheless amputated from our personal fullness until the moment of the resurrection, because we will not have the body that is the natural expression of our soul.

There is something very interesting in this regard concerning the apparitions of the saints. I do not speak, of course, of the Virgin Mary, who is in heaven with her body, or, a fortiori, of the risen Christ. But in the history of the Church, certain saints have appeared, and they have done so in a corporal manner. They do not have a body, but they can only appear to human beings on the earth in a bodily way. God gives them a bodily appearance so that they can manifest themselves to us and so that we can enter into communication of the senses with them.

This shows us just how much we need the bodily dimension in our relationships with other people, even in the case of the saints. The communion of the saints with those who have returned to the Lord normally passes only through prayer and faith, that is, through the invisible realm. This is why any human attempt at spiritualism, the evocation of the dead by the medium of a living person, a table, or any other object, is deeply against the order established by God. Only God can restore (momentarily) to a deceased person the appearance of his or her body, if he thinks that it is good to do so. But we cannot, in any case, evoke any of the dead or enter into mediation with them using inevitably magical intermediaries. The communion of saints remains necessarily in the realm of faith. God, on exceptionally rare occasions, can allow manifestations through signs perceptible to the senses, but he alone can do it, not us.

We Were Created for Eternal Life

The other profound reason for our anguish in the face of death is that we were created by God not for death but for eternal life, in our soul and in our body. This may seem contradictory to what we said above, namely that man is naturally mortal. Yes, it is true, man is naturally mortal; and by nature, by their bodily nature, by the bodily part of themselves, our first parents, Adam and Eve, were naturally destined to die. But God created them in a supernatural condition of grace, which normally meant that they would not have died and humanity would not have known death. They would have known a passage from the life of history, from the temporal life to the eternal life. It would still have been a "death" in the sense that there would have been a transition from one state to another, something like what faith tells us occurred in what is referred to as the "dormition" of the Virgin Mary at the end of her earthy existence. But even this analogy is only a very distant one, because the Blessed Virgin, in her association with the redemption of her Son, shared at the same time many aspects of fallen humanity; hence, she too endured suffering. So it is not really possible to affirm that the form of "death" that she knew was what our first parents and all humanity would have known if they had not sinned but followed the ways of God. For an innocent humanity, this "death" would not have been linked to the trials and sufferings of Christ's redemption and paschal mystery, as was the case for Mary, but instead it would have been a passage from the love of that which is limited to that which is unlimited, from the temporal to the eternal, a transition, an ecstasy, an exit from the limits of a history that evolves and changes constantly into the eternal present moment of God.

This is what we were destined for, and it is very surprising to see how much this aspiration towards paradise is still inscribed in the heart of man. There is in us a nostalgia for paradise, a humanity that was not made for disease, degradation, and death. This idea haunts our minds. We have a nostalgia for the lost paradise, for a condition of grace where the life of the Spirit, having permeated our soul, would have been reflected in our body that would finally have been introduced into the eternal life of God. This is what has been lost by original sin and all the subsequent sins by which we ratify the first sin. And yet this condition remains like a secret wish in the heart of man.

Today we often see our contemporaries recoiling before death or revolting against it. If God accepts the cries of revolt uttered by Job in the Bible, as well as those of our contemporaries today, it is because he understands that man carries within himself this nostalgia for Adamic grace, in which the entire journey of humanity ought to have been accomplished. Indeed, original sin was not something inevitable. Contrary to what people often think, it was not simply due to the limits of created beings. Original sin was actually a terrible catastrophe, a great rejection of grace by human freedom. Sin can never be part of God's design. What is part of God's design is freedom. It is our freedom that can commit sin, but sin as such has never been inscribed in God's design. God assumes it and responds to it by giving us his Son to save us, but it is not something he wanted, either directly or indirectly. God did not in any way take sin into account in his original purpose. That shocks our spontaneous representations. We think of God as having a kind of prevision where he anticipates the future, as if he himself included sin in his primordial purpose. But, in fact, the relationship between the Lord and time is much more mysterious than that, for every moment of our free decision is seized in the eternal present moment of the Lord, in his purpose. And this design of love and grace, as God proposed it to Adam and Eve, did not involve sin, and therefore did not imply death.

By Sin Death Entered the World

Saint Paul in the Epistle to the Romans is able to declare, "sin came into the world through one man, and death through sin" (Rom 5:12 ESV). The death of human beings; the death of animals does not at all have the same status because it does not damage an immortal soul. Their death is part of a cosmic order of bodily beings animated by a principle of life that is purely sensory or animal, therefore mortal. The death of a human being, on the other hand, injures a person whose life principle is an immortal soul. That is why it is so painful to die. That is why God wanted to keep man free from death in paradise. This original paradise was not yet heaven, but it was a journey towards heaven through time, a journey that would not have gone through the corruption of death, but which would have enabled us to pass by a sort of ecstasy of body and soul from the history of this changing world towards eternity.

Basically, is it not to this that we all aspire? Paul, in one of his epistles, employs a very eloquent expression, saying that we would like to be not "*unclothed*," but "further clothed, so that what is mortal may be swallowed up by life" (2 Cor 5:4).[1] Such would have been the case in paradise: we would have put on immortality over our bodily garment. While now, alas, we must first go through

1. My paraphrase of the ESV, which reads in full: "For while we are still in this tent, we groan, being burdened—not that we would be unclothed, but that we would be further clothed, so that what is mortal may be swallowed up by life." Once again, Jean-Miguel telescopes the biblical thought.

decomposition. Our body, as it is now, will be reduced to dust. This is the meaning of a liturgical paraphrase of a Bible text that was once always said and that can still be used when the priest imposes ashes on Ash Wednesday: "Remember, man, that you are dust and that to dust you will return" (cf. Eccl 3:20; 12:7).[2]

Yes, by way of our body we come from dust, from the matter of the cosmos, and our body will return to the cosmos and be dissolved in it. Whatever veneration we may have for the relics of the saints, whatever the devotion with which we pray over the tombs of the dead, we must not allow the pictorial representations that have been given of the resurrection to mislead us. After thousands of years, nothing remains of most bodies. Everything has fallen to dust. The resurrection of the dead will not involve bones leaving the graves and coming back to life. As for relics, they are the traces of what was the body of a saint in his historical reality, and the sign of the relationship that keeps his separated soul connected to his particular body. But his relics and bodily remains do not constitute the indispensable foundation of his future glorious body.

We Will Rise with the Same Body

Since this is the case, how is it that at the resurrection we will rise with our very same body? This will happen precisely through the soul, which was created for a particular body. The soul is the "form" of an individuated body, the principle that confers upon the body its structure, its organization, even its physical configuration. When the time comes for God to allow our souls to inform matter in the glorious state, it is this same body that will exist again. It will be the same, since it is the soul that was created for it that will give it its identity. It will therefore be our very same body, but it will not be in molecular continuity with the body, perhaps already damaged by infirmities or handicaps, which was deposited in the tomb and which then dissolved into the earth.

2. Jean-Miguel is referring here to the liturgical phrase in the Roman Missal derived from the biblical text.

Indeed, starting from the moment of "metaphysical" death, when the soul is separated from the body, we cannot say that the corpse is really a body. It still appears as such, but, in fact, it is no longer a body. From the moment when the soul goes away, the body is nothing more than a decomposing corpse. We can try to conserve it and artificially seek to maintain its outward appearance, but left to itself it decomposes very quickly. We can embalm it like the corpse of Lenin in the mausoleum of the Red Square, but it is no longer a body, it is a mummy. The only bodies in the true sense of the term are living bodies, alive through the life of the soul. The corpse only represents mortal remains. It is a trace of the body, nothing more.

Thus, as we have said, the resurrection of the flesh will take place because God will restore to our souls the ability to inform matter. But this time it will be matter in a glorious state, and not in a state of evolution, subject to generation and corruption, but a matter that will be fully spiritualized. We have no way of imagining what this is. It is one of the mysteries of the apparitions of the risen Christ or the Virgin Mary. The matter of which their body consists and the contact that the seers had with it when they gazed upon it or touched it, all these things are very disconcerting for us because they belong to the physical conditions of the new world, a world of which we have absolutely no experience. We do not know what a corporeal, cosmic world in an eternal state is like, because the cosmos as we know it is in a state of evolution, of generation and corruption, of history which is in continual transformation.

This new cosmos in its state of eternity already exists in the risen body of Christ, sacramentally present under the signs of the bread and wine consecrated in our Eucharist. Jesus is present under the appearances or species of bread and wine, and because his body is that of the Risen One, he can be present in all the Masses and tabernacles of the world without being divided into pieces. It is a glorious body whose physical properties do not correspond at all to those of our world, so it cannot be broken apart, injured, or diminished in any way. It can be present in different places because it is like an irruption of the new world into our old world. The body of the Virgin Mary, who through the mystery of the Assumption is associated with her risen Son, is also of this nature.

Anxiety at the Loss of the Body in Death

But while waiting for the resurrection to occur there is a gap that provokes repugnance and anguish: our body must descend into the tomb and undergo corruption, decomposition. It is always disturbing to see skeletons, for example, in the catacombs in Rome, and to say to oneself: here are the mortal remains of beings whom we believe are alive with God and whose only trace here below are these bones which are headed ultimately for decomposition in the cosmos. It is also very disturbing to witness the reduction of a corpse, something that can be quite macabre. It makes us realize that only a few years after their death, the bodies of our grandparents or great-grandparents are reduced to dust.

This gap is very frightening, not only for the nonbeliever, for whom it is obviously a kind of leap into the total unknown, but even for the believer. The latter can say to himself, "I am going towards God, but I will exist without my body, I will no longer have an historical existence, I will not exist anymore through my body in this world which is in the continual process of 'becoming.'" All this inevitably gives rise to a great deal of anxiety, related to the very structure of our being: it is precisely our profound belief in the immortality of the soul that can make us anxious at the thought that this soul will be deprived of its natural mode of expression, its natural field of activity.

How else can we communicate with each other except through our bodies? Even our thought process and our will have their points of departure, as Thomas Aquinas already pointed out, in the knowledge that comes from the senses; our spiritual acts are therefore very much related to the body. We do not know concretely what it will be like to think and to love without our body. We are so used to having feelings, sensations, perceptions; even our most spiritual activities draw on bodily sensations through all the subtle alchemy we call the psyche. The psyche is not the soul, properly speaking, but something like an "outcrop" of the soul that collects the sensory information received by the body. The psyche elaborates this information and places it at the disposal of the soul, which then makes of it the fulcrum of its acts of intelligence and will. To be faced with a non-bodily existence, even if it is only an inter-space between the moment of death and the moment of the resurrection, can therefore be a cause of considerable anguish. This accounts for what we can call the "metaphysical" fear of death, which must be distinguished from another fear that is purely human or psychological: all the anguish experienced in the face of the sufferings that ordinarily precede death. We are afraid of that which prepares us for death and leads us there. But death itself is the source of a properly metaphysical anxiety that we are unable to completely suppress. In this perspective, we can no longer resign ourselves to being a simple cog in the cosmos, in accordance with the conception underlying the various forms of Asian wisdom; we cannot persuade ourselves that the loss of our body will simply be a liberation. For us, the body is not a tomb that imprisons the soul. On the contrary, the fact of being deprived of one's body frustrates the soul of something on its own level, the spiritual level. Death cuts the soul off from its normal conditioning and from its corporal mode of expression and places it, as it were, in a "violent" state.

The Great Denudation of Death

Christian theology, as it is expressed in the writings of Thomas Aquinas, has never sought to erase the violent character of the situation that occurs from the moment of our death until the general resurrection. True, this amputation of our body will be compensated in the supernatural order by all that will happen in the area of our relationship with God, as we enter on a much deeper level into the communion of saints. But knowing this cannot suppress the metaphysical anxiety caused by the prospect of being a soul without a body, that is to say, a person amputated of his natural integrity. That is why it is so important to accompany the dying.

It is only gradually that God prepares a soul for the great poverty of death.

To leave one's body, to be dispossessed of it, is a terrible privation. The body is the one thing that is really our own; you can lose everything else, but as long as you have your body, in a certain sense, you still have everything. The loss of the body is the nakedness that Job was referring to: "Naked I came out from my mother's womb, and naked shall I return" (Job 1:21 ESV). This refers not only to the nudity of the body that is stripped of its faculties, but also to the absolute nudity of the soul deprived of its body. This represents a terrible form of poverty not only for the dying, but also for the healthcare team that tries to fight the disease and realizes that it must capitulate. For some, this sets off the chain of aberrant and contradictory reactions that we have already discussed: first therapeutic obstinacy, then euthanasia. These two things derive from the same order of logic, from the same dream of omnipotence, a refusal to accept the natural role of death. A natural death is rejected first by trying to postpone it indefinitely, as if healing could inevitably be produced sooner or later by medical techniques. And then, finally, it is denied through a decision to inflict death or have death inflicted upon oneself by anticipation, precisely in order to avoid submitting to it. This is a form of suicide, an act of despair.

We can absolutely not evaluate the degree of consciousness and guilt of those who commit acts of this type: it is something very mysterious, and it is certainly not for us to judge. But from an objective point of view, these are acts of extreme despair. They are only understandable, although even that hardly makes them justifiable, because of the great metaphysical anguish into which death plunges us and which can make us forget sound moral references. Around a dying person there is often a real whirlwind of panic. This is one of the areas in which our Christian faith should help us give a true witness to our world. A witness of peace, gentleness, serenity, which is not the same thing as fatalistic resignation. The Christian faith is not resigned. Often it is said that we must take things with resignation. But serenity is not resignation. People resign themselves to what they consider to be an impersonal, fatalistic destiny. We, on the contrary, are serene in the face of death because it is something that we know comes from the hand of God. We accept it also because it has a natural dimension. We have lost the Adamic state of grace; we must therefore submit to the law of nature; we have abandoned humanity's state of primordial grace through original sin and through all our own personal sins that ratify the sin of our first parents. Therefore, we need to accept death with serenity, saying with Job, "The Lord gave, the Lord has taken away: blessed be the name of the Lord" (Job 1:21 ESV).

If we must die, it is due to the fact that we broke the original covenant with God, a covenant that would have shielded us from death. But we know that in the covenant renewed by Christ, we are promised eternal life. It will be given to us, first in our soul from the moment of our death, and then in our body through the final resurrection. We know all this in faith. It is therefore in the night of faith that we must go through death. In Saint Thérèse of Lisieux's last conversations, published under the title *To Enter into Life*, we can follow what it was like to go through agony for a twenty-four-year-old tuberculosis patient, treated by the, for us, still primitive methods of medical science as it existed at the end of the nineteenth century, without all the means that we have today for relieving people who go through a similar ordeal. This leads us to reflect on the attitude we must have with regard to the physical pain which often occurs during agony.

In any event, the process of physical decline or degradation is the lot that we all carry within us, and the problem we have to face is ultimately a metaphysical one. The pain relief procured by modern medicine does not really alter the basics of the problem. On the other hand, it is conceivable that, precisely thanks to the conditions of a more humane death offered by today's medical science, patients who are approaching their last hour can more lucidly face up to the great metaphysical act that they are called to accomplish without being inhibited by physical pain, which, if not sedated, would confine their consciousness almost completely to the level of pure animality. It is therefore an important duty to relieve as much as possible the physical pain of the dying so that it does not reduce them to an infra-human state.

Relieving Pain so as to Help Cope with Suffering

Death is an awesome trial that we cannot avoid. Today, in the face of those who, as we mentioned above, desperately resort to things like therapeutic obstinacy or euthanasia in an effort to evade and deny the anxiety inspired by death, we Christians must face up to that anxiety with serenity, while coordinating our efforts with those who strive to help others die in a way that is fully human, relieving their pain and helping them to avoid all that can be dehumanizing in death.

In the field of palliative care, a great deal of extremely commendable research is being done to find ways of combating pain but which do not psychologically disconnect the person: thus morphine is definitely to be preferred to those treatments called "lytic cocktails," which tend to put the patient in a vegetative state. Of course, it is not clear what people treated with products such as these actually experience in the depths of their consciousness. The only thing that is clear is that these products have the sinister advantage of keeping patients in a passive state where they won't cause much trouble for the medical personnel! Fortunately, today, we have developed ways of combating pain that allow the person to remain, as far as possible, in his right mind so that he can meet death in a lucid manner. I firmly believe that we do not have the right to "steal someone's death away from him." This expression was coined by Bernanos, and it is very true indeed.

It is therefore necessary to give the dying person as much relief as possible so that he can enter death without being alienated by pain that, otherwise, would completely confine him to the physical level. Someone who is subjected to unbearable pain can no longer express the profound dispositions of his soul (unless it be exceptionally for brief instances, thanks to a strong influx of supernatural grace). He becomes imprisoned in his pain, he becomes nothing but pain. It is scandalous to note that sometimes certain

Christians, and even Christian caregivers, under the pretext of the faith, show a tremendous indifference to pain (to that of others, of course, because when one is a patient oneself, one sees things quite differently!). We hear them say with resignation: "This is something we must all go through. It is the way to merit going to heaven."

Such an attitude is positively abominable. I personally love the figure of Saint Veronica, who is not mentioned in the Gospels but who, according to tradition, came with her veil to wipe the face of Jesus when he was on his way to be crucified. This woman did what she could to offer Jesus a little bit of relief. And the Lord knows how much a dying person can be touched and moved by even this modest gesture of someone wiping and refreshing his face! . . . We must do all that is possible to bring relief to the dying so that they can still feel themselves to be human. Because, just as when people fall below a certain degree of misery, they become subhuman, and the church tells us that we have no right to leave part of humanity in a subhuman situation, so too, when a person reaches a certain degree of pain, he becomes subhuman. There are people who have actually thrown themselves out of windows because they could no longer stand the pain. They were no longer in their right minds, they no longer belonged to themselves, they were completely overwhelmed by pain.

This helps us to understand the remark made by Saint Thérèse of the Child Jesus to Mother Agnès, her older sister who was also the prioress of her convent: "Take care, dear Mother, when you have sick people in the grip of such violent pain, not to leave poisonous medicines near them. I can tell you that when someone suffers to this degree it would take only a minute to lose one's mind and then it would be easy to resort to poisoning oneself." We must remember that the one who speaks these words is the same Thérèse who appeared not long afterwards, in the last photograph taken just after her death, with a face transfigured, as if God had decided to give a presentiment of what her resurrected face would be. The photo gives the impression that she did not go through any agony, and yet, in fact, she experienced a terrible one, as terrible as any agony can be.

Today, we must fight against pain on the strictly medical level, and Christian doctors should be on the front lines of this combat. True, pain can also be the place where grace works. But let us not tempt God, let us strive to relieve as much as possible our brothers and sisters who endure pain, just as we would seek to alleviate their poverty. And let us not be too quick to preach to others, saying: "Blessed are those who suffer, blessed are the poor . . ." It is all too easy to give this message to others when one is on the other, comfortable side of the barrier! This is in no way an authentically Christian attitude. We cannot choose pain for others. To choose it for ourselves can sometimes be admirable if God's grace inspires us to do so. If a person voluntarily refuses to take painkillers in order to offer himself in love, this can perhaps be a way of achieving heroic holiness. But we have no right to refuse giving sedatives to others.

At the time when a person must pass inevitably through the supreme spiritual test constituted by the great denudation of death, when he is called to enter into this absolute nakedness involving the loss of his body, at the moment when he is about to arrive before the everlasting Lord in total poverty, without his body but with the entire weight of his sins for which he needs to ask forgiveness and mercy, I really do not see how extreme physical pain can, in itself, bring him any additional advantage. If it is possible for us even in the least way to calm that pain so as to allow the person to face as spiritually as possible the decisive moment of death, I see absolutely no reason why we would not do so. There is no doubt that God can work through even the worst pain endured by a person, as happened with Thérèse of the Child Jesus, for whom the pains of agony became an ultimate purification in view of holiness. But God has also given us intelligence and scientific knowledge, and it is our primary duty to put these in the service of everything that can humanize the life of man. And there is a definite duty to humanize death.

We are not made to die in just any haphazard way. This was the major intuition of Saint Mother Teresa who, with very few resources, created homes for the dying in India. She knew very well that she would not be able to save the lives of most of her patients. She founded not hospitals, but homes for the dying, so that people could die in a more dignified, human manner. This was all that she and her sisters were able to give. But they at least provided a loving, caring human presence, along with certain gestures of comfort and consolation. Unfortunately, we often fall short of this in our overly technicized but inhuman hospitals.

Fortunately, today there is a movement in the opposite direction with the discovery of palliative care. It is too bad that Christians up until now have not been attentive enough to this, for it is an important duty of mercy. It is very important to allow a person to die well. When someone is going to retire, we try to give him the most favorable conditions for entering into this new stage of life. It is even more necessary to give everyone the most favorable conditions for dying, since from a spiritual point of view, this is the most important moment of a person's life. If we can, we must therefore strive to relieve the dying person of pain that will not help him to face the profound denudation that death demands of him. I myself was fortunate enough to accompany cancer patients who benefited well from medicine procuring pain relief, and I witnessed a number of very lucid, beautiful, spiritual deaths. These people were not devoured by pain and could die in a fully human way. Spiritually, these were very intense moments. Such moments probably occur in other cases as well, but unfortunately they can be hidden under intense pain or psychic disconnection.

3

The Redemptive Value of Suffering Offered in Love

Illness as a Test with Regard to the Scandal of Evil

Medically incurable illness is a harbinger of death. Man's revolt against illness is part of his legitimate revolt against death. Illness, along with the suffering that it entails—moral suffering and, more often than not, physical pain as well—announces that death is close at hand or at least not very far away. This is why illness is often the occasion of a revolt against evil.

Accidental death, which occurs suddenly, is such a shock that it does not necessarily leave time for revolt. People who have survived a serious automobile accident where they saw themselves on the verge of death do not usually claim to have experienced at that time any sense of revolt. They tend instead to experience a kind of accelerated playback vision of their entire past in the few moments of the accident. Illness, on the contrary, because it leaves much more time and involves a slow deterioration, which in itself is like a physical beginning of death, often provokes revolt, especially when it is not simply a passing illness, but one whose outcome seems, from a medical point of view, likely to be fatal.

We have here a particularly painful type of revolt. The sick person is constantly torn between two things. On the one hand, he clearly sees that death is for him a natural thing, since he has an animal body that wears itself out, ages, and deteriorates over time. But on the other hand, he has a perception of the immortality of his soul, and this, in turn, seems to be a kind of obscure promise inscribed in his being, that his body itself will also participate in immortality.

It is, therefore, above all with regard to illness that man is confronted with the scandal of evil. During the illness the person often goes through two phases. The first of these is to make God responsible for all the evil, to reproach him for the illness and to say to him, "Why have you allowed me to become sick? If you are good, if you exist, how is it possible that I should suffer, that I should be sick, that I should be deteriorating and approaching death?" Then a second stage comes where the person turns the accusation against himself. Realizing how futile it is to accuse God by making him responsible for evil, the person starts blaming himself, "In what way did I offend the Good Lord so as to deserve having this happen to me?" How many times have we not heard words such as these in the mouths of the seriously ill? "Why has God punished me in this way? What sin have I committed?" And as we have all committed sins, it is easy for us to find all sorts of sins which seem to have earned for us this punishment.

Caught between Revolt and Guilt

We often oscillate between the two attitudes mentioned above: on the one hand, we accuse God of being the cause of our illness, of having created the world all wrong: "Why," we say, "did he make a world where it is possible to suffer, to die?" On the other hand, we blame ourselves, saying, "If I am sick, if I am slowly getting ready to die, it is because I have sinned. I am being punished."

In the first attitude we come up against the scandal provoked by the suspicion that God, the source of all things, God, whom we spontaneously think of as being pure goodness, might be the author of evil in the world. And yet, on more careful analysis, such a reproach proves to be completely unfounded. To ask why God did not render us incapable of dying is to ask why he created us with a body. Death is linked to our corporeality; our animal nature does not entail immortality, at least not in that which concerns the body. On the contrary, everything in our body announces that we are gradually wearing away, that we are subject to fatigue and death. To ask God to have created us immortal would be to ask him not to have created us human. If we accept the fact that we are human, we must accept our mortality. And yet we cannot accept it because, as we have seen, we carry within ourselves a certain immemorial reminder of paradise, a state of grace that ought to have led us to eternal life.

God created us mortal simply because it was not possible for him to create us immortal. God can make either circles or squares, but he cannot make square circles, he cannot simultaneously create two things that are contradictory one to the other. He cannot create a *naturally* immortal bodily nature. But within us there remains the remembrance of paradise, that is to say, a state of grace in which corporal mortality, not by nature but by grace, would have been bypassed and transfigured. In the person who suffers, there remains a painful longing for paradise. Although this attitude is in part a revolt against God, as we see in the book of Job, it is not nearly as bad, not nearly as harmful, as the attitude of guilt through which we turn the accusation against ourselves.

Not that the attitude of guilt is completely erroneous. It contains an element of truth: if there is death in the world, it is because of the sin of humanity. If death has entered the world, it is because man has sinned. But the error in the attitude of guilt comes when I begin to imagine that my death, my suffering, my sickness, are directly a punishment of my sin, a punishment proportioned to my faults. And thus an anxious search begins: "What fault could I have committed in order to deserve so severe a condemnation?" But at the same time we are also confronted with a number of deaths which are extremely scandalizing and revolting, like the death of children, or that of particularly good people who are cut off in the prime of life. Here one is forced to note a very great disproportion between the sufferings, the trials, the diseases that befall these people, and their personal guilt.

The ambiguous interrelationship between the guilt of sin and death proves that the feeling of guilt, although it is a sign of sin, is certainly not the measure of sin. In general, when we feel guilty, it is because we have sinned, but the sin we have committed is not necessarily commensurate with our sense of guilt. It is the astonishing but constant experience of many confessors to see how some sins that are more serious than others from a moral point of view are admitted with much less a sense of guilt: sins against charity, against justice, sins of indifference to neighbors, hardness of heart, are sometimes not even mentioned in confession because people fail to discern them. It is not that they are seeking to hide these sins; they simply don't see them. On the other hand, when it comes to the sins of the flesh, the slightest weakness is experienced by most people with a great deal of shame, as something very difficult, painful, and humiliating to confess.

This does not mean that there is no culpability involved in the sins of the flesh, but we are obliged to recognize that there is often no measure between the actual gravity of these sins and the sense of guilt they inspire. In the same way, the relatively weak sense of guilt inspired generally by faults against charity and justice, which are nonetheless at the very heart of God's law—"You shall love God with all your heart, all your soul and with all your strength, and your neighbor as yourself" (cf. Deut 6:5)—is not an exact measure of the gravity of these sins. Of course, if we had not sinned, we would not feel guilty. But we also sin sometimes without feeling any guilt. The feeling of guilt is only an indication; it needs to be taken into consideration, but by itself it is incapable of adequately measuring the gravity of any particular sin.

Co-responsibility of All Men with Regard to Sin

It is not according to the measure of our guilt or of our fault that we suffer the consequences of evil. Just as there is a communion of saints, there is also a communion in the consequences of sin. The virtues and merits of a saint are reflected on the whole mystical body and are beneficial not only to himself but also to others. In the same way, the sins of each one of us harms the entire mystical body of Christ. There are little ones, the poor, the "innocent," upon whom participation in the cross of Jesus weighs more heavily, even though they have not necessarily sinned in proportion to the suffering that befalls them.

It is the book of Job that confronts us with this mystery. Job doesn't claim not to have sinned. He simply states that there is no measure between the sufferings that have come upon him and his personal sin. His friends still remain in the earlier, Old Testament mentality prevalent before the book of Job: God, it was thought, rewarded the righteous, filling them with blessings while punishing sinners with misfortune. This is in fact true, but only at the end of our life when we are judged by God: then we can say that there will be an absolutely perfect retribution. But as long as we are still on our way in this world, we are living under a system of "co-redemption." In this system, people who are less sinful than others find themselves more closely associated with the mystery of the cross of Christ. Job could not yet be aware of this, because he was anterior to Christ. But the book of Job somehow resonates with the mystery of the Suffering Servant. It is very interesting to note that chapter 53 of the book of Isaiah on the Suffering Servant, which announces the redemptive passion of Christ, and which is historically located either at the end of or just after the Exile, indicates a growing awareness of the problem of evil. And this is precisely the central theme of the book of Job, which also dates from after the Exile.

In a way, each of these two texts reflects the actual experience of Israel. Indeed, the nation of Israel, which suffered through the siege of Jerusalem by King Nebuchadnezzar, followed by seventy years of deportation and servitude in Babylon, became very much aware of having sinned and felt that it was being punished by God for its sins. But it realized at the same time that it was suffering a double punishment for its crimes, as the prophet Isaiah says,

"Comfort, comfort my people . . . Speak tenderly to Jerusalem, and cry to her that her warfare is ended, that her iniquity is pardoned, that she has received from the Lord's hand double for all her sins" (Isa 40:1 ESV). Double punishment, because Israel is a nation of priests and is therefore mysteriously associated with the redemption of the world. The people of Israel receive a double punishment: true, they have sinned, but they are asked to bring into the mystery of the Redemption a double contribution, which is not proportionate to their faults and which places on their shoulders a portion of the sin of humanity. This will appear in the figure of the Suffering Servant, who represents both the people of Israel and the mysterious person who is to be born of Israel, the redeemer destined to save God's chosen people together with all humanity.

When considering the link between our faults on the one hand and our sickness, suffering, and death on the other, we must always take into account the mysterious co-responsibility of all mankind, which works in both a negative and positive direction. Due to the fact that by our faults we have weighed down the cross of Christ, the only truly righteous and innocent one, we have, in the mystery of his mystical body, also rendered heavier the sufferings of those who are "innocent." We speak here of "innocence" only in a secondary and derivative sense, because no one is entirely innocent except Christ himself. Even the Holy Innocents, even small children, are not completely innocent to the extent that they are already caught up in a history marked by original sin; for this reason they all carry latent malice within themselves, even if they have not had the time to activate it.

By our faults, we may have mysteriously caused this or that suffering, such and such an illness, this or that unjust evil, to weigh upon others in the communion of the saints. Others have perhaps suffered double punishment because they bore some of the burden of our sins, while we during that time were carefree, leading a pleasant life. When, on the other hand, we are touched by misfortune ourselves—and who has not been, is not, or will not be in one way or another, since we are all mortal?—it is possible for us to find there an opportunity to share in the burden of others. From a certain point of view, this can be a very comforting thought. And it is not at all a form of masochism. Suffering is obviously a terrible thing, and no one should love suffering merely for the sake of suffering. But with regard to justice, there is a certain relief in the realization that we will not always have to back off from our responsibility for sin by putting the entire weight of our faults first of all on Christ, the only righteous and innocent one, and secondly on others, all those who with Christ carry the burden of the sin of humanity.

Why should I necessarily always enjoy good health, immediately find the wife or husband whom I can truly love, have children while others do not because they are sterile, succeed perfectly in my professional life? Why take all this for granted as something normal to which I am entitled, to the point that when something breaks down, I enter into rebellion? Did I fail to realize that while everything was going well for me, during those years when I did not even feel the need to concern myself with the question of evil because the experience that I had of it was reduced only to small annoyances, was I not aware that during all this time the poor and the innocent were shedding blood, sweat, and tears? Then, finally, when the Lord comes knocking on our door with sickness, trial, failure, humiliation, or with the various forms of physical or psychological wounds that life can bring us, does he not in some way convict us of unconsciousness, carelessness, and indifference?

When this happens to us, shouldn't we rather breathe a sigh of relief, saying to ourselves, "At last the Lord is taking me seriously and is inviting me to pass over to the side of those who are carrying the cross with him, in the manner of Simon of Cyrene who was recruited to help Jesus?" We know that it is Christ alone who really carries the cross. But in him, unceasingly, even today, a certain number of his disciples are called very concretely, very precisely, very painfully, in their flesh or in their spirit, to bear the cross. Why should I remain seated until the end of my life alongside those who, in a spirit of pettiness, selfishness, dryness of heart, and in a blind appetite for the pleasures of life, contribute to consolidating and reinforcing the burden of sin that has oppressed humanity ever since the original fault of our first parents?

If an illness can help to make us aware of sin, it ought not do so in terms of culpability. One ought not to ask: What sin have I committed that is proportionate to the trial that has befallen me? Such a question makes no sense because everything, our sin as well as our holiness, enters into a mystery of communion. There is an extraordinary phrase of Saint Paul that is used during the funeral liturgy: "No one lives to himself, and none of us dies to himself" (Rom 14:7 ESV). Through our sin and through our holiness, we are in an invisible but extremely real communion with all men, without exception.

God Is Not Unfair When We Suffer

Each one of us in turn is therefore called to enter into this redemptive mystery of Christ and bear some of the weight of other people's sins. But our trials do not occur in proportion to our own sins. The justice of exact retribution will only be accomplished after our death. At that moment, to each one will be given according to the measure of his or her love. It will be an extraordinary type of justice because we will be filled according to the capacity of love that our free will developed during our lifetime in response to divine grace. The one who has developed a capacity of love comparable to the size of a thimble will be filled to the size of a thimble. Whereas the one who has developed a capacity comparable to that of an immense basin will be filled with the love of God like an immense basin. This will be an absolutely perfect form of justice, because it will be dictated precisely by the measure of our heart. What will be our "weight of love" (as Saint Augustine calls it) when we leave this world? It is according to this measure that we will be filled with heavenly bliss. Of course, if during this life our liberty is able to grow in love, it also has as a risky counterpart the possibility of totally hardening itself against love, thus bringing into play the mystery of damnation. But in heaven it is our measure of love that will be our measure of bliss, our eternal happiness.

Let us have no fear: in the end, there will be no injustice. But from now until then, in this world, it is not the measure of justice that presides over the retribution of men, but the measure of redemption and the communion of the saints. And although there is no retribution proportionate to our actions, when we are associated with the mystery of redemption through sickness or through ordeals of various sorts, it is important to realize that we are not being treated unfairly. Because all of us have sinned, and in this sense it is normal for us to receive the wages of sin, which is death. None of us can say, "I have not sinned, and therefore sickness must not befall me." This is not true; even the little child who has just been born is already a bearer of sin by that mysterious complicity with sin which is the negative side of the communion of saints. For this reason, even the death of a little "innocent" one is not an absolute scandal.

If we were to close ourselves up in an individualistic perspective, all this would seem incomprehensible and scandalous. But God did not create us as isolated individuals randomly placed one next to another. Saint Paul tells us that we are members of one body, members of one another (Rom 12:5). There is between us not a mere juxtaposition of individuals, but an exchange, as if between the members of the same organism, and this creates among us an interdependence. We are therefore indebted to the entire body of humanity and responsible for the life of this mystical body of Christ that is in the process of being built. By our faults we annihilate graces that were intended not only for ourselves, but also for all others, and we can sometimes put our finger on this fact concretely in our lives. Most often, by refusing grace that was destined for us, we close a valve, and this in turn dries up an entire sector of our human relationships in which these graces should normally have flowed. Whenever we sin, we sin not only for ourselves, but we sin also for others. When we understand this, we have much less desire to sin, because, oddly enough, it is easier for us to love others than it is to love ourselves. It is very difficult to love oneself. Often one learns to love oneself by loving others. There are many things that we would readily do for others but would not do for ourselves.

We are called to relay divine grace to others. When we cut ourselves off from the influx of grace, other people suffer the consequences: most often those people who are closest to us, but also, in a much more mysterious but no less real way, people we do not even know but who are enveloped in the same current of love that embraces all humanity.

From the Wages of Sin to an Offering of Love

And thus, we do not receive sickness, the preparation for death, as a punishment proportionate to our faults. It is indeed the wages of sin, but a wage that calls us to enter into a redeeming mystery where, precisely, our faults will begin to be saved. If we would only accept to give more than we imagine we owe, if we would accept to enter into a larger gift, our sufferings would be much easier to bear. This is a discovery that is often made by the sick who go to Lourdes. The great miracle of Lourdes, it has been said, is not miraculous cures. These are very important as a sign of God. But the great miracle of Lourdes is that the sick who go there realize, when they come in contact with each other, that they are not only suffering for themselves, but that they are suffering for one another and for the entire world. It is this redemptive perspective of their sickness and suffering that gives meaning to their ordeal and brings them out of their isolation. Guilt always tends to lock us up within ourselves, whereas the perspective of the communion of the saints liberates us to the same degree and opens our heart.

When we see that through suffering, sickness, trial, and failure, we are called to enter into a mystery of communion and that Christ asks us to join him in bearing the burden of others for their salvation and for ours, instead of feeling oppressed and overwhelmed, instead of judging ourselves to be horrible sinners who have been rejected by God, we should feel called by the Lord to exercise the priesthood shared in common by all the baptized. This priesthood was inaugurated by the people of Israel, to whom the prophet Isaiah said that God had made them pay a double punishment for all their crimes. In the same way, we are called to give, to give doubly. Starting from the moment when we hear that call, we are happy to be able to give more. We deeply regret having misunderstood the love of God, the sufferings of Christ, and the sufferings of our brothers while we went on living in a reckless manner, committing acts of sin, sins of harshness, of selfishness, and of indifference towards our neighbor. When, on the contrary, we become capable of loving our neighbor, we are happy not only to repair to the extent of what we contributed to the damage, but to overcompensate in the mystery of the communion of saints.

Redemption is a mystery of overcompensation. It is not simply a question of giving what you owe, but rather of entering into the spirit of forgiveness, forgiveness that gives more than what is required, which gives over and above. When we enter into the mystery of forgiveness, we are made ready in the Lord Jesus to suffer that which we have not deserved. As soon as we enter into this mystery of suffering, through illness among other things, we are asked to give more: we are asked to give ourselves.

This makes it possible to escape the false dilemma: Is God guilty because I suffer? Or am I guilty? No, God is not guilty! But I am not guilty either to the extent of my suffering, because the true measure of my fault is known only to God, and I must never try to evaluate my fault by imagining that the extent of my suffering corresponds to the punishment that sin has earned for me. On the contrary, when God allows me to be associated with the cross, he shows me that he does not take into account my fault, since he invites me to participate in the redeeming mission of his Son, who calls me to the greatest form of intimacy, inviting me to drink from his cup, to take up his cross. It is the opposite of a rejection; it is the sign of a choice and even of a kind of predilection.

Called to Give Everything

All this cannot be said immediately to a patient. But we can whisper it to ourselves. In any case, we sometimes hear patients say it themselves, and I have on occasion been a witness to this. I recall the case of a mother who died while giving birth to her eighth child, leaving eight orphans and a husband who suffered from tuberculous. She pronounced words which astounded me, and I can understand how some people would even be scandalized by them. To a person who, when she was dying, expressed compassion, she answered, "No, to suffer is a privilege." She had the absolute certainty of being associated at the highest level with the redemptive work of the Lord. In no way was it masochism, a morbid taste for death or suffering. Nor was it an attitude of irresponsibility with regard to her children and her husband. But, called in this excruciatingly paradoxical way to give her life, she responded immediately, she put everything—the children she left behind, the child who was born, her tubercular husband—into the hands of God, convinced that since he was inviting her in so inescapable a manner to make a total gift, he would take care of all that she had to leave. She knew in whom she was putting her faith, and she was not disappointed.

I do not say that this can be demanded from everyone, and moreover God does not require it. If someone were to die under these same conditions, shouting her pain and even her revolt, God would not condemn her any more than he condemned Job. But it is good for us to know that there are some people who surrender their lives like this even under such extreme circumstances so that we can say to ourselves that there are still a number of Christians who have heard, in all its seriousness and in all its gravity, Jesus's call to take up the cross and follow him. This is what Jesus said to Angela of Foligno, a great Italian mystic of the Middle Ages: "It is not merely for play that I loved you." It is a very serious matter to be loved by God. It is not just to make us laugh, it is to lead us through death into eternal life.

Sooner or later, God will ask us to give everything, but of course only according to our capacities, because the Lord is merciful. As the saying goes, "For the sheep who has been sheared, the Lord scales down the intensity of the wind." And luckily for us! God will not ask of us the impossible, and if he demands something that seems impossible, he will give us the necessary graces so that we can accomplish it. Thus we see people who carry crosses much heavier than what we would have thought them able to bear, and they themselves are the first to be astonished. I have often been told, "If I had known in advance that I would have to go through such a trial, I would never have imagined that I would have the strength to do it. I do not know where my strength comes from." Even nonbelievers sometimes say and experience this, for grace is given to everyone. As believers we are able to know from where our help comes. But anyone can see that there is a state of grace involved when one is called to enter the mystery of the cross and give one's life.

We Can All Offer Our Lives

It is good for us to know that there are people who have totally given their lives. No, it is not because of guilt, and I see proof of this in the writings left to us by Jacques Fesch. He appears to have forgiven those who condemned him. It's not that he judged himself to be innocent, but he realized that, in any case, there was a disproportion between his crime and the punishment that was imposed upon him. He was required to give his life, to accept living as a man condemned to death awaiting the night of execution. This was a terrible ordeal that was not in proportion to the harm done to the person (a policeman) whom he had killed in an unpremeditated manner. It is terrible to have to go forward day after day so surely towards death.

Jacques Fesch sensed perfectly well that Jesus was asking him something that went far beyond the simple expiation of his crime. Much more was required of him: he was asked to give his life. They did not simply limit themselves to taking his life, as might have happened if he had perished immediately after having killed the law enforcement officer in an exchange of shots with the police. But it was quite another thing for him to have to enter into this inexorable march towards death, to see it coming from afar, to have to accept it. And that required of him forgiveness. He knew that he was getting what he deserved in justice, like the Good Thief who was crucified alongside Jesus and who said, "For us it is justice, we are paying for our deeds, but he [i.e., Jesus] has done nothing wrong" (Luke 23:41).[1]

Jacques Fesch did not deny that it was justice for him. But this human justice now required of him something that was much more than the price of blood, and which was the free gift of his life. Jacques Fesch gave this gift of his life just as a terminally ill patient can do, or as the mother mentioned above was able to do. He did not feel unworthy to give the gift of his life in a spirit of forgiveness towards others, although he himself was condemned to death for manslaughter.

The worst murderers, the worst scoundrels, the worst sinners, by offering their sufferings and giving their lives, can go far beyond the redemption of their faults. They can literally become saints. The most evident example of this is the Good Thief in the Gospel who was the first to enter paradise with Jesus. Jacques Fesch constantly carried in his mind the image and example of the Good Thief, the first saint, the only one who was canonized not by the church but by Christ himself, the one concerning whom we have been given the certainty from the mouth of Jesus himself that he entered paradise first, since he entered with Christ at the time of his death ahead of all the righteous of the Old Testament whom Jesus was to seek in Hades on Holy Saturday.

What an extraordinary privilege! God, through the mystery of illness or suffering, calls us not only to atone for our faults, but, even more so, to enter into the mystery of forgiveness, of extra-compensation, where we are happy to give for others, to give superabundantly, to give over and above that which could be required of us in justice. We will always be scandalized by the mystery of suffering as long as we remain in an individualistic perspective and try to weigh what we owe with exact scales. Perfect justice is not of this world. There is certainly a duty of justice in our human relations, and we must continually strive to attain a higher degree of justice. But the ultimate justice, the mystery of retribution, is for the hereafter. We see that illustrated in the parable of Lazarus the

1. Paraphrase of ESV. The original: "And we indeed justly, for we are receiving the due reward of our deeds; but this man has done nothing wrong."

pauper and the rich man (Luke 16:19–31). It is, by the way, terrible to note that the rich man only committed a sin of omission: he did not see Lazarus, he failed to see the poor man at his door. But it was an enormous sin of omission which lasted an entire lifetime, and it hardened the rich man's heart, extinguishing in him any capacity to love to the point where it would seem that he ultimately incurred damnation. Yes, omission can be a deadly sin. Omission can lead us to damnation. The sin of omission is the lack of love; it is even in a certain sense the most serious, the most insidious form of the lack of love.

Since retribution is not of this world, illness, suffering, and trial are not commensurate with our sin. They are the measure of the sin of humanity and the measure of the redeeming love in which we are asked to participate. Why does he require this of us? Why is it being required of me in particular to suddenly pass from the situation of the rich man to that of the pauper?

To that question there is only one answer: because others have done it before, because Jesus did it first, and because they did it to save the sinner who I was and who I still continue to be in a part of myself. It is necessary that some people give more, that they forgive, that they give over and above the measure of justice. Such is the mystery of redemption that contains in itself the ultimate secret of suffering. Suffering in itself is not redemptive: considered alone, suffering is something quite appalling. It would be masochism to say that suffering as such is redemptive. But suffering is the privileged place where the call for redemption resounds. And redemption is love. In suffering, we are called to love and to give more. It is like an open door. In 1984, Pope John Paul II wrote a very beautiful apostolic exhortation on "The Christian meaning of human suffering" (*Salvifici doloris*). In it he declares that suffering is a particularly favorable occasion for us to hear the call to give our life in love, to refuse always being on the side of those who profit, who ignore suffering, who back off from their responsibilities. Why should we always remain on their side, we who are sinners like them?

The Grace That Works through Suffering

This is what is at stake, this is what must be shown to the sick, this is what we must remind ourselves of on the day when we too enter these great trials. But only God can give us the grace to perceive it. While I was a chaplain at the cancer center I mentioned earlier, most of the people I visited did not practice their religion. Some were not even believers. Nonetheless, they welcomed my visit, because it offered them the opportunity to talk to someone who was neither a part of the medical team nor a family member. As the chaplain, I represented for these people someone with whom they could speak truthfully. Not being a medic, I was not exactly aware of their clinical condition. But I was also not a family member who dissimulates, to whom one often dissimulates, and to whom the doctors sometimes lie. There are situations of inextricable lies, as a patient once told me, "My family lies to me so that I will not feel bad and I lie to them so that they will not feel bad." With the chaplain, it was possible for them to speak in secret, both believers and nonbelievers.

What struck me most in the itinerary followed by these patients was the way in which grace worked in them, even among the nonbelievers. Of course, these latter were unable to give it the name "grace," but I observed how they changed over weeks and months, preparing themselves without knowing it for the kingdom of love. They did this above all by entering into the mystery of forgiveness. They often arrived in a state of revolt against their fate, against God, with all their projects for the future shattered. Some were quite young, others were in the prime of life, the rest were elderly, but no one is really ever ready to accept the prospect of a death that suddenly appears to be relatively close at hand. At first, these people tended to be extremely aggressive, sometimes even violent, insulting the nurses, complaining that the care was poorly done and that it hurt when they were pricked with needles—then, in the course of weeks and months, with interruptions, because they would often have to come and go for chemotherapy, one could see the spirit of forgiveness growing in them. They would mentally pass in review their entire lives, in the solitude of their room. (Each patient had a single room, which is often considered a luxury in hospitals, but which can also impose a formidable loneliness.) For all of them, believers and nonbelievers alike, it amounted to a veritable retreat.

They were obliged to confront their entire past, with all their resentments and frustrations. One had the impression that they were purified little by little through the mystery of suffering. Everything that was bad in them, the revolts, ambitions, frustrations, grudges, detached itself from them. They entered into the mystery of forgiveness, compassion, gentleness, understanding. Those who, when they first arrived, would insult the nurses because (according to them) they gave injections poorly, appeared at the end, if not in a painful, at least in a very uncomfortable situation with veins so badly bruised that it was no longer possible to administer intravenous injections. But having reached this point, these same people would often say to me, smiling, "You know, the nurses are so nice! They try to do everything they can for us." Their vision of things had changed. This helps us to see that although suffering by itself is not redemptive, it is a doorway to redemptive grace, and that it somehow softens the hardness of our heart so that we can be permeated with divine grace.

It is along this road that we must accompany patients who are terminally ill. The entire way cannot be revealed to them all at once, except in exceptional cases, thanks to special graces. But we need to be there to gradually help them decipher the mystery of redemption into which they are entering. We need to accompany them and help them realize that the circumstances in which they find themselves are for them an opportunity for self-giving, something which, in the final analysis, is probably the deepest desire of the human heart, a desire that is so hard to fulfill. If we are often oppressed by a feeling of having failed in our life, it is generally because we have not really been able to give ourselves. But, quite frequently, it is in the last stage of our life, in the final illness, in our agony and death, that we are able in truth to offer this total gift.

We must not deprive patients of this opportunity by grossly deceiving them. I remember once seeing (and indeed, I often witnessed similar episodes) family members at the bedside of a dying person, trying to reassure him in a falsely casual tone, saying, "You'll see, in two weeks from now you'll be gallivanting around, you'll be able to go camping in the mountains!" while they knew full well that the one they were talking to was terminally ill. The patient knew it too, but he felt obliged to play the game so as not to hurt his loved ones. But as soon as the visitors left, he confided to me, "It's terrible to have to play such a comedy!" He sensed that in his family circle, they were afraid of death. Of course, it is plainly out of the question to say bluntly to someone, "You are going to die"; but on the other hand, we've got to avoid falsely consoling him with gross and blatant counter-truths. These are unbearable because the patient, on one level or another, senses perfectly well that people are lying to him.

On the contrary, it is necessary to help the patient realize that the end of his life is the last word, that which will give meaning to everything else, and that he will be able to make of it his "final bouquet." In fireworks, the "bouquet" is the last explosion, the most beautiful, the one reserved for the end. The end of our life must be that bouquet, the free act through which we truly give ourselves. This must not be taken away from us, it would deprive us of something much too important. It is obvious that when we are ill, we need to receive relief so that we will not be alienated by the pain. But no one should steal from us this gift of our life, this offering of the metaphysical suffering involved in losing our body, of entering into the great nakedness of death, of leaving the sensory world in order to go to God. It is our last act of human dignity in this world.

4

The Mystery of Death Illuminated by Christianity

Through Illness God Prepares Us to Meet Him

EVERY ILLNESS IS A preparation for death, and we never know for certain which illness will cause our death. People diagnosed with clinically fatal conditions sometimes die of some other illness or in an accident. There are also people in apparently good health who die suddenly of cardiac arrest or of a stroke. I have known of cases where this has happened to some while they were caring for or accompanying the dying, preceding, as it were, their patients in death.

I would often bring up this fact to the patients I visited. Those who were terminally ill were convinced that they only had a few weeks left to live on this earth. But I would tell them, "Whatever our state of health, our life is in the hands of God." "No one knows the day or the hour," as Jesus says (Matt 24:36). When they objected to me, "But you are going to live, while I am going to die," I answered them, "Yes, it is likely that I will survive you, but I could also be hit by a car when I leave this hospital." We must not try to know the day of our death, or evaluate the time that remains for us to live. We must, however, always be ready for an encounter with God, and this is something quite different.

God can provoke this ultimate encounter suddenly, at the most unexpected moment, since he himself has warned us that he comes "like a thief" (Rev 16:15 ESV). We must be careful to understand this expression correctly. It is not about a thief coming to rob us of life, but rather about a savior who comes to snatch us away definitively from the world of sin in order to bring us into eternal life. Death is the moment when we are met, rejoined, and supremely overtaken by the redeeming grace of Christ's salvation. Any other interpretation of the term "thief" used by Jesus would be absolutely despairing and revolting. In this final moment of our life, the grace of Christ focuses upon us as if through a magnifying glass and concentrates in one last assault to make us topple over, not into damnation, but into bliss with God, into eternal life.

This salvation is not given to us by death (for death itself is not salvation), but it is given through death by the one who is the living God. This salvation is already being prepared, and it is often announced through the illness that leads to death. This is already a direct preparation for the encounter with God in the last passage, in the Passover of our death. For this reason, fatal illness carries with it a grace of redemption and conversion that the Lord put there. Even in cases of violent death, it has sometimes been found that people who were going to die suddenly—in an accident, for example—had a kind of presentiment of death. In some people, a sort of change of interior disposition was noted, a change that foreshadowed a secret conversion of the soul.

This change is much more obvious, of course, in the case of a long-term illness that leads to death. I have witnessed many cases where patients have undergone an amazing change of attitude, and this has happened not only among believers, who could more easily express it in the terms of faith, but also, as I have said earlier, among nonbelievers, those who hardly believe at all, or those who do not practice their religion. All this leads me to the firm conviction that there really is a great multitude of those who are saved.

It is true that as long as we are in perfect shape physically and mentally, as long as all our selfishness and our will to exercise power and control over things continues to enjoy free rein, we are sometimes assailed with doubts concerning our salvation, our own and also that of others. At such moments we tend to ask ourselves: How will it be possible for us to fall into the presence of God when we die, if our hearts remain so hard?

The Multifaceted Work of Grace in Those Who Are Ill

Contact with patients who are heading towards death gives the opposite impression. One observes the work of grace, one can literally see it over the weeks and months. And this is true not only for the small number of those who experience a conversion to the faith during the last stage or even the last hours of their life.

I make a distinction here between a conversion to explicit faith on the one hand, and a conversion to love on the other. Catholic theology maintains that conversion to the faith is absolutely necessary for salvation unless it comes up against invincible ignorance that obscures the intelligence in us, without any ill will on our part. But we will be judged on love. True love, charity, is the presence of the Holy Spirit, and this presence is given by the redeeming blood of Jesus, who died for every man without exception. We know by revelation that there are absolutely certain and sure channels for the transmission of this redeeming love by the Holy Spirit: these channels are the faith, the sacraments, the life of the church. But we do not know the multitude of paths for grace that the Spirit can invent so that the heart of every person may be touched by the blood of the redeemer.

I recall one young mother who died, leaving several children. She was not a believer, but neither was she officially an atheist. She did not practice any religion and God was not at the center of her life. She was nevertheless a very good mother and a fine, good-hearted woman, although not exempt from shortcomings. In particular, she had a very difficult relationship with her father. It was not a profound opposition, but during the entire period of her illness, which was an extremely painful form of cancer, her aggressiveness was focused on him. Her father got on her nerves; she never really ever said mean things to him, but she showed annoyance every time he went to see her at the clinic. In the days leading up to her death, there was, as is often the case, an improvement in her condition, and the day before her death she was completely lucid.

Those who visited her then found her overflowing with tenderness and love for everyone. The last words she uttered were to say to her father, "You look very handsome with this tie, it really suits you so well!" Her parents left her, she fell asleep for the night, and after waking up the next day, she died in the space of a few moments. Her last words may seem laughable and banal. I think, however, that they were in this instance like God's key opening the door of eternal life in her soul. She could only use that innocuous phrase, since she had no other, to express the love that had triumphed in her heart. Persons who are nonbelievers have no words other than ordinary everyday ones to express that they have tipped over in favor of love. In this woman's heart, love needed to overcome this small obstacle in her relationship with her father. By giving her the ability to pronounce these last words, God gave the sign that her heart was like a ripe fruit ready to be plucked for the eternal kingdom. And after that, she died very rapidly indeed.

A Long Spiritual Combat

From someone on the path of an illness, the thing that often delays death is a lack of abandonment to love; for example, the refusal to forgive or to receive forgiveness. Before they can die, some people must wait to receive a word of reconciliation, a word of forgiveness, which is indispensable for the peace of their soul, and which is the place where they will be able to surrender themselves to God. Death is an act of abandonment to love. Those who are believers know who is love: they know that it is God and that he has taken on the human face of Jesus. Those who do not believe do not know this consciously, but they nevertheless feel it: they sense an inner movement in their heart that leads them to love.

Among the patients who were stricken by cancer, there were, as I have said, those who were still in the full momentum of life, men who were young or in the prime of life, people in complete possession of their means, in full self-affirmation of their personality. I saw men who held a great deal of power in their hands: business executives, social and political leaders, but who were all of a sudden wounded by the prospect of death, and who were obliged to enter the long solitary retreat that periodic visits to the anti-cancer clinic represented for them. I say "solitary retreats" because deadly disease, even if it is not contagious, creates a relational vacuum around the patient. It was there that these powerful people had to face themselves. When they arrived, they were in full revolt, that is to say, still in their domineering attitude. And then they would go through the period of guilt.

Finally, I saw them in the period that, for hospital chaplains, announces the nearness of death: living in a kind of peace with humble abandonment. This is most often the sign that the Lord is at hand. The Lord really does come "like a thief"; he comes when we do not expect it, but he prepares the soul for death. He wants to obtain our conversion to love, a conversion that each person expresses as best he can, with the words and the lights that God has given him. I have observed people who experienced rapid flashbacks of their entire lives and who gradually gave up hatred, the desire for revenge, grudges, so that they could end up achieving forgiveness and love.

Abandoning Pride

One of the deaths that struck me most was that of a young actor, a stage performer. His situation was all the more tragic because, already at the time, his cancer could have been cured, but there had been a mistake in the treatment at the beginning. Due to this, the young man, who must have been between twenty-eight and thirty, was inexorably doomed to die. The first time I went to his hospital room, he accepted my visit just to be able to talk to someone, as the vast majority of the sick do, to the extent that we listen to them rather than do the talking ourselves.

He quickly told me, "When I arrived here, the illness had taken me while I was in full activity, in the fullness of life, at the height of success in the theater. I led a life that could not be more joyful, and then suddenly everything was blown away. All those who surrounded me in the rather factitious world in which I lived deserted me overnight. Nobody came to see me, to the point that I phoned one of my closest friends and said to him, 'You know, cancer is not contagious!' But I understood that the contagion does not necessarily have to be biological. It can also be psychological." What his friends did not want was to see the coming of death, something that would already force them to face their own death. The young man went on with his story: "Then I rebelled against my friends. I began to hate them, thinking that they were continuing the happy life I had led myself, and that they had completely abandoned me when I was alone dying in this hospital."

Finally, this patient entered into a description of his spiritual experience: "Then I literally went down to hell, I lived through an experience of hate and damnation. I was nothing but hatred for all these people who had adulated and courted me, and who now abandoned me. A few days before this, my parents had come to visit me and my mother, without saying anything to me, slipped a rosary under my pillow. That night when I went down to the bottom of hell, at one point, I slipped my hand under my pillow, touching the rosary. At that moment an inner voice said to me, 'Let go of your pride and hatred and pray!' I began praying the 'Hail Mary' and 'Our Father,' and I could feel the hatred taking flight and leaving my heart. From that time on, I found peace and even a kind of joy. I wrote to my friends, I phoned them. I took an interest in them, in their lives; and I began to feel myself in heaven."

This young man died soon afterwards, in peace. He had been taken back from the clinic to his parents' home, where he died very gently. In departing from this world, he left those who had accompanied him with a great deal of light. It is very curious, but in this last stage of his illness, he no longer suffered even physically. He simply grew weaker and weaker. He was able to pray for all his friends who had turned their backs on him, he could look at them as children of God who had gone astray, like he himself a few years earlier. He was already in the kingdom of God. This young actor had a Christian background that re-emerged and enabled him to clearly express the work that grace was accomplishing in him. But I have also seen similar transformations in people who were only able to express what was happening in very banal, ordinary words, but who nonetheless died like this young actor, in an abandonment to love.

The Pressure of Eternal Life

"We will not die of death, we will die of life," said Teresa of Ávila, whom we quoted earlier. She herself died in a sort of rapture of love. We die because the kingdom of God enters our heart, because eternal life is already present in us. We fall into that life, just as a ripe fruit falls from the tree. This is what I have seen so many times with the patients I accompanied: when I would see them suddenly change, become patient, gentle, understanding, shedding all kinds of aggressive behavior, this generally indicated that they were very close to death. Their change was a sign that the Lord was already coming for them.

As one gets closer to death and therefore also to eternal life, there is a sort of concentration of the action of God's grace on the person who is going to die. This growing pressure of grace in the heart is expressed by each person in his own particular language, gestures, and habits, but it is something easily identifiable by those who surround him.

The sick need to be able to talk with those who accompany them. If they are not believers, they will not necessarily need to talk about God, because, except in cases of extraordinary grace, it is almost impossible to catch up in a few short months or weeks on a lifetime of ignorance concerning matters of the faith or to eliminate a deep-seated religious disaffection that may have its roots in negative past experiences. Nevertheless, everyone needs to talk, to pierce all the pockets of bitterness, of sadness, to express their regret for the sinful acts they have committed. I listened to the confessions of many more people than those to whom I was able to give sacramental absolution. Almost everyone felt the need to get rid of the things that weighed on them. Many were not ready for sacramental confession because they lacked the explicit foundations of faith. Grace did not begin by slowly leading them in that direction because God was in too much of a hurry. The important thing was that they come to contrition and repentance, surrendering to the authentic desire to love that God was inspiring in them. This of course could not happen without them seriously re-examining their lives and engaging in some deep personal questioning.

Among patients of this type, I recall one young father of a family. He was a self-employed mason, and part of his work was done off the books, illegally. His aim was to earn as much money as possible in order to build his own house, so as to have a more respectable residence. This man had literally "worked himself to death." Although he had a wife and two children, he had completely sacrificed his family life. Returning to his past, he said to me, "If I come out of this alive, I will reconstruct my life in a totally different way. I will accept to live more poorly, I will give up the ambition which till now was the only aim of my life: to earn more and more money. Now I understand: when I return home, I will take the time to go out with my little boy, to talk with him, to be with my wife. They missed me, but I lived only for my work, my goal was to make money. Of course, I was doing it for them, but still, I missed out on that which is essential."

On the other hand, one sees, in very rare cases, people who harden and do not manage to die. Their death becomes a terrible struggle because, precisely, God wants to save them, and he does not want to take them in the hardened state in which they are closing themselves. Here we enter the mystery of the last moments of life. We do not know what is transpiring there. When the combat seems very dark, it suggests, from the outside, the possibility of damnation. The possibility but never the certainty. Because one feels at the same time the vehement action, the pressure exerted by God's grace.

Those who are hardening themselves already begin to live in hell, because hell is simply the hardening of love. When this happens, love burns like a fire, becoming for them something unbearable. God loves all his creatures without exception. There is no such thing as a place outside his love, which would be hell. Hell is the same love of God that rebellious creatures, hardened against him, transform for themselves into a fire of damnation. Those who harden themselves against love have an anticipated experience of damnation.

And indeed, all of us experience this on a small scale. Whenever we harden ourselves against love, cutting ourselves off from communion with our neighbor, giving ourselves up to hatred, we enter into a presentiment of damnation. On the contrary, when we enter into true love for our neighbor, into charity, we already have a foretaste of the happiness of heaven. We have all already tasted a tiny sample of what hell is like, and a tiny sample of what heaven is like. These foretastes are given not only to believers but to everyone. The unbeliever will not be able to designate it as "heaven" or as "hell," but there are other words that mean the same thing: "It's hellish, I'm in revolt, in hatred, in bitterness, in an unbearable despair."

The Presentiment of Eternal Life

Do the graces of conversion that accompany illnesses at the approach of death ever reach the point of becoming true mystical experiences, constituting a kind of anticipated perception of the hereafter? This is a vast topic which has become an object of curiosity. In his book, *Life after Life*, Dr. Raymond Moody launched discussions on this topic. He questioned a number of people who had experienced clinical death, a brain-death coma, and who came back to life. I do not agree with the more or less spiritualistic interpretations he gives; one senses that he bathes in an atmosphere of spiritism. It is easy to see how one could argue from this in favor of things like the migration of souls, reincarnation, or spiritualistic communication with the dead. But at the base of all these testimonies, there is certainly a reality. The people Dr. Moody interviews all express what they experienced in a very similar way, and this seems to me to converge with my experience in accompanying the dying. It is quite common that patients who have approached or (in very rare instances) even reached clinical death talk about these experiences, either because they returned to consciousness after a very deep coma or because, without yet being in a coma, they were in a state that seems hallucinatory.

Often a patient will resolutely stare at a particular point in the room as if he saw something or someone. I am talking about patients who are not in a coma but who are very close to death. Some actually speak to someone whom they see. One patient I knew was very much afraid of death. At one point, he said, "I see my mother in heaven. She is saying to me: 'Do not be afraid, you are coming to me.'" After this, in his final days, the man was totally at peace, constantly staring at the same corner of the room where he had seen his mother. This "visitation" of loved ones who are already with the Lord is something that is known to happen at times.

The Heavens Opened

Alongside those who talk about what they have seen when coming back from a coma, we must mention the much rarer instances of people (notably, certain saints) who before death speak of seeing heaven while fully awake. They experience a kind a presentiment of eternal life, although they have not yet died. First of all, we should recall the testimony of Saint Paul, who "was caught up to the third heaven—whether in the body or out of the body I do not know . . . and he heard things that cannot be told, which man may not utter" (2 Cor 12:2–4 ESV). After Paul, we find this kind of experience among a certain number of martyrs. They experienced states where they saw the heavens opened. This is what Stephen exclaims at the time of his martyrdom: "I see the heavens opened and the Son of Man standing at the right hand of God" (Acts 7:56 ESV). He saw the heavens opened before being injured, before anyone had thrown a stone. Some martyrs of the first centuries claimed to see the glory of God before being put to death. And the witnesses of those scenes were sometimes converted on the spot because they too saw the glory of the Lord and therefore joined the martyrs in order to share their fate.

We are told of other mysterious phenomena, such as when martyrs seem not to have suffered under the tortures to which they were subjected. There is, for example, the beautiful story of Saint Perpetua and Saint Felicity, two martyrs of Carthage. Because one of them was pregnant, they waited for her to give birth before putting her to death. She gave birth in her prison, and as she screamed in the pains of childbirth, her executioners laughed at her, saying, "If you scream like this today, what will it be like tomorrow when you will be fed to the wild beasts?" But she answered, saying, "Tomorrow, it is Another who will be suffering in me."

Saint Maximilian Kolbe, who was imprisoned in a hunger bunker of Auschwitz, underwent a similar experience. Those condemned to these bunkers were deprived of water and therefore slowly died of thirst, with all the horrible suffering that this implies: dehydration, tetanus, contractions of the muscles . . .

Father Kolbe succeeded in getting the group of inmates who were with him to sing God's praises. Although in the other bunkers, horrible cries were heard, Father Kolbe transmitted to his companions the strength of Christ. He himself remained alive for two weeks, the last survivor, and he had to be put to death by a "nurse" of the camp who gave him a shot of potassium. This nurse later testified that he was pierced by the last look of Father Kolbe resting upon him: a look of extraordinary love, peace, and forgiveness. Saint Maximilian's victory over death and the powers of hell was thus total. His look gave the impression that he had not suffered, or rather that Another had suffered in him.

Ritual Prayers for the Commendation of the Dying

There is something here that is ineffable. We are looking at the moment immediately preceding death, when the realities of eternal life are anticipated in this life. It is not that the soul has already left the body to go to eternal life, but it is eternal life itself that comes to the soul. It is heaven that approaches. God, Jesus Christ, the Virgin Mary, the angels, and the saints come to the dying person. This is exactly what the church evokes in the prayers for the commendation of the dying, which today, unfortunately, are only rarely used. These are splendid prayers and they include, among other things, the beautiful Litany of the Saints where the angels and saints are asked to come and meet the dying person. These prayers are still used in monasteries, but unfortunately they are only rarely practiced in families. They are not easy to do because it is usually necessary to start them over and over again and keep them going. This requires a great deal of dedication on the part of those who surround the dying person. As no one can be sure when the end will actually come, people need to take turns saying these prayers.

There are two liturgical acts that the priest must accomplish for the dying person and that are prescribed in the ritual. The first of these is the plenary indulgence that accompanies confession and communion received as a viaticum to prepare for death. The indulgence gives the believer the merits of the communion of saints in the mystical body of Christ, so that he can pass directly from this life to heaven. At the moment of death it entirely purifies him of anything he may still have needed to atone for because of his sins. It is very moving for a priest to be able to open in this way the gates of heaven to someone in the name of Christ. I have done it a number of times, especially for people who could not die. Although they had already received the sacrament of the sick and the Eucharist in viaticum, they died only after receiving the plenary indulgence for their faults.

The second liturgical act is the recommendation of the soul to God, in which the priest commands the soul, saying, "Go forth, Christian soul, from this world in the name of God the almighty Father, who created you, in the name of Jesus Christ, Son of the living God, who suffered for you, in the name of the Holy Spirit, who was poured out upon you, go forth, faithful Christian. May you live in peace this day, may your home be with God in Zion, with

Mary, the Virgin Mother of God, with Joseph, and all the Angels and Saints." By these solemn words, the church signifies to the soul that it has completed its mission on earth and that is now being entrusted to the Lord. It sometimes happens that people die at the very moment when these words are spoken to them.

Sometimes there is an obstacle that prevents the dying person from giving up his soul: this can be because the heart has become hardened and is plunged in darkness, or simply because there is a fear of dying. In this case, the powerful words of the church ritual can help him to let go. Those who are less afraid of death die more easily. Whereas those who are extremely frightened of death cling desperately to life, even if this is now only a miserable form of survival. The dying need help in order to die.

Here we should note that the sacrament of the anointing of the sick is not essentially linked to the prayers for the dying. It is not in itself an "extreme unction," as it was almost always called in the not-too-distant past. It is intended first of all for the sick in order to provide them with the graces of strength and healing necessary to fight against and overcome their disease. But in the final stages of life, it can really become an *extreme* unction because it reaches the soul at the point where it is anchored in the body, freeing the soul from its instinctive attachment to the body so that it can adhere above all to the Lord, who is calling it to enter into eternal life.

The terrible anguish that death inspires because of the total stripping it represents for the soul can only be overcome by an act of surrender and self-giving. Jesus before dying on the cross uttered these last words: "Father, into your hands I commit my spirit" (Luke 23:46 ESV). The prayers for the dying, together with the anointing of the sick, when this is administered as extreme unction, are there to help us follow Christ on this path.

Ultimately Consenting to Love

All these presentiments of heaven in someone who is dying are there to complete the work of conversion that is being accomplished by grace. They put the person in a state where his perception of the hereafter is so keen that the only possibility, the only danger or risk of damnation for him, would be if at that moment he chose to commit the sin against the Holy Spirit, against the one who is love in person. For that which is announced in the graces of conversion, and which then culminates in the mystical experiences of the end of life, is the perception of the kingdom of love. To damn oneself is to refuse this kingdom of love, to refuse it for oneself and for others, to blindly refuse the fact that God is love. It is only when man is about to die, and when he arrives at this ultimate perception of the love of God, that he has the fearsome possibility of posing so radical a refusal, a refusal that constitutes damnation.

Despite this danger, we must believe that the power of the redemptive grace of the blood of Jesus is immense, as well as that of all the communion of saints, and all this weighs heavily at that moment on the soul of the one who is going to die. The soul undergoes the life-redeeming pressure exerted by the merits of Christ and by the merits of the saints who are the members of his body and who have adhered to him by loving to the point of giving their lives. This is why in the prayers for the dying, the saints, the Virgin Mary, the angels, the apostles, the martyrs, the fathers of the church, the holy monks, the great founders of religious orders, the mystical saints, are invoked in the Litany of the Saints. They are invoked because they are the mystical body of Christ who, at that moment, is exerting pressure on the soul so that it will freely accept to enter into the kingdom of love. At the same time, though, the devil and his evil angels unleash themselves, exerting pressure in the opposite direction.

This is why the fight of agony can be particularly dramatic in those who have long closed their lives to love, as well as in those who have closed themselves to faith despite being given in their hearts the real possibility to believe. The case of an unbeliever who did not believe because he did not have the opportunity to know or recognize the truth of God's revelation and who simply stayed outside of the faith is very different from that of the unbeliever who has had inner callings to the faith but who has refused them out of pride. Not all unbelievers are proud; some are very humble. I recall one father who lost his three children. On the occasion of the death of the last of these, he said, "I do not feel God, I cannot conceive of him with my intelligence or with my sensitivity, but that does not mean that he is not in me. God can be in us without our realizing it." These words, spoken in so difficult a circumstance, indicate an extraordinary degree of humility, which is perhaps a very real form of holiness in someone who is an unbeliever. Only the gaze of God can penetrate the secrets of hearts. But there are also those unbelievers who have received graces of faith and who have refused them. Some who later converted confessed this refusal with a great deal of regret. They recognized that they had failed to respond to the graces of faith out of pride, or out of vanity, fearing what others would think or say.

The Fight at the Frontiers of Eternal Life

There is undoubtedly a struggle in this final phase that precedes clinical death and that can also continue between clinical death and metaphysical death, that is to say, the actual separation of soul and body. We have some testimonies from the few who have experienced clinical death and who have come back to life. In general, they come back transformed. I remember the testimony of an evangelical pastor. As a result of an automobile accident, he had been in the state of clinical death, during which time he had a mystical experience. When all this occurred, he was not yet a believer, but this experience provoked his conversion. When he came back to life, not only did he have faith, but from that moment on he resolved to give his life to God.

From a distance, death seems to be a dark threshold. Indeed, it is the "narrow door," according to the expression used by Jesus in the Gospel of Luke (13:24 ESV). And Job says, "Naked I came from my mother's womb, and naked I shall return" (Job 1:21 ESV). We leave this world more naked than we entered it, since when we leave, we will not even have our body. This narrow door is an obscure threshold, and yet, as one approaches it, either for oneself or when accompanying the dying, one realizes that, like a half-open door, it allows some light to filter through. Those who have been close to someone who is dying, if they looked with a sufficiently attentive heart, have seen rays of eternal light filtering through in one way or another.

André Frossard, in his book *God Exists: I Have Met Him*, tells how one day, as a total unbeliever, he entered the Chapel of Adoration and Reparation on the rue d'Ulm in Paris. There, he writes, "in a sudden moment, I saw the light of heaven . . . It was a bluish light . . . I perceived heaven for just a few moments, and when I left the chapel I was a believer." I myself have witnessed similar phenomena with the dying. These occurrences show us that the Lord can overcompensate, by mystical graces, the handicaps from which a person has suffered during his lifetime with regard to the faith. The Lord does this for a select few before their death, while they are still fully conscious and are able to talk about it. But this is not the case for everyone. Does he do it for the others in the lapse of time that separates clinical death from metaphysical death? Not everyone comes back from a coma to tell us. In any case, it is on love that we will be judged.

My opinion is that God allows us to know these exceptional cases so that we can believe the words written by Saint John, when he says at the moment of Jesus's entry into his Passover on the evening of the Last Supper: Jesus, "having loved his own who were in the world, he *loved them until the end*" (John 13:1 ESV; emphasis mine). "Until the end" means that he loves us until his death and also until our death. With all the riches of his redemptive grace, he reaches out personally to us in death, he joins us as soon as the prospect of death is explicitly outlined on our horizon. People who have come back after having been briefly between life and death remain transformed by this experience. They do not necessarily have the words to express it, but there emanates from them a soft serenity, a particular kind of patience, which gives us the impression that they are no longer quite of this world. They already belong to the kingdom of God. This is true of each of us since "the kingdom of God is within" us (Luke 17:21 KJV), but most of the time we stifle it and end up forgetting it.

In the final analysis, it is the supernatural life itself that frightens us the most. In the fear of death, there is not only a legitimate anguish due to the prospect of having to accept the metaphysical nudity represented by the loss of the body. There is above all a fear of the kingdom. The ultimate graces that prepare death and anticipate eternal life serve as a mystical taming of the soul so that not only does it no longer fear the kingdom, but actually desires to enter it. All the people interviewed by Dr. Moody were unanimous in saying how much they regretted having to return to life here below. They felt attracted to the infinite space of love, light, and peace of which they were given a glimpse. The reality was still veiled to them because they were not actually dead; otherwise, they would have seen God face-to-face. The graces they experienced still belong to the realm of faith and not of vision. They involve presentiments of eternal life that are probably necessary for some people, especially those who have not had any previous experience of an explicit supernatural life. For a believer who has already tasted a certain mystical life, the simple heart-to-heart contact with the Lord, which does not necessarily belong to the order of extraordinary experiences but which is much more discreet, can usually be sufficient. Thérèse of Lisieux died in an extremely dark night of faith, but with such tremendous love! She died saying simply, "O my God, I love you!"

5

The Last Act of Liberty at the Moment of Death

Clinical Death and Metaphysical Death

How is it possible to distinguish between clinical death and metaphysical death? Clinical death is an empirical definition of death. It is fixed in an approximate and partly conventional way, according to both medicine and law. When can it be declared that someone is dead? This issue is particularly important when it comes to things like organ harvesting. Clinical death has had different legal definitions. It is currently defined by two consecutive flat electroencephalograms. This could change with the evolution of scientific knowledge. But clinical death will always remain an approximate determination of real death.

We have already seen what can happen at the deep level of the soul, even during periods of brain-death coma. But people who have experienced the state of clinical death and have returned to life are not "resurrected." They did not die a metaphysical death; their soul was not yet separated from their body in an irreversible manner. Clinical death is almost always followed by actual death, but in a very few cases the person comes back to life. This is not a "resurrection," but instead resuscitation *in extremis.*

This shows that something does happen between clinical death and metaphysical death. There is an interval of time, which can be of shorter or longer duration, between the two. That is why at the moment of death, the tradition of the church prescribed prayers around the dying person, not only until he gave clinical signs of death, but even afterwards. It is true that in the past, it was more difficult to determine whether or not a person had actually died clinically. This could have terrible consequences, because during certain epidemics some people were buried alive and then woke up in their graves! In normal times as well, the church asked that prayers be continued even when it was sure that the person was clinically dead because of uncertainty about the moment of the separation of the soul from the body. The continuation of prayers is particularly opportune in the cases of persons whose agony has been very difficult, not only from a physical point of view, but also spiritually. These people were perhaps not entirely ready to enter the kingdom of God, or to open themselves to the mystery of love.

The face of a dead person at the time of clinical death is often still extremely tortured, especially when there has been a great deal of suffering. It is only afterwards that the expression changes and becomes peaceful. Yes, something does happen after clinical death. According to a Spanish proverb, "It takes a half an hour after death before one sees the soul." The meaning of this is that at the moment of the real death, the metaphysical death, the moment when the soul leaves the body, it leaves its last expression on the face, an expression that is like a last farewell. It is this ultimate expression that is so striking in the photo of Saint Thérèse of the Child Jesus on her deathbed. The lapse of time between physical death and metaphysical death is obviously very difficult to measure. The church will never say how long it can last. In all likelihood, it is variable according to each person.

Intercession for Those Who Enter Death

I have heard, without being able to verify it, that Marthe Robin received private revelations from Christ on this subject. Private revelations, of course, are by no means binding on the faith of the church, but as long as they do not contradict that faith, everyone is free to receive them with respect and devotion. According to this private revelation, real death can occur, depending on each case, between half an hour and something like seven hours after clinical death. The delay would vary according to the preparation or non-preparation of the person for death. The extreme case is that of those whom a sudden death takes by surprise. During the time interval between clinical and real death, many things happen, because the soul must prepare to give its ultimate consent to love, or else refuse it. This can involve an immense spiritual battle.

Marthe Robin, who relived the agony of Christ every Friday, entered into spiritual combat with the demon while in a state of agony. She prayed and offered herself constantly for the dying, especially for the most abandoned among them. She thus had a certain inner experience of what agony is like. Even if one day, as seems probable, Marthe Robin is canonized, her spiritual experiences or revelations will never be imposed as an object of the faith. No Catholic will ever be required to believe them. They are, however, morally guaranteed by a woman whose life reached a high degree of holiness, even though the church has not yet officially beatified her.[1] It is very striking that she was aware, thanks to a

1. The cause for the beatification of Marthe Robin, who inspired the foundation of the Foyers of Charity communities and who died in odor of sanctity in 1981, was examined by a Vatican commission. Among the experts who participated was the well-known Carmelite spiritual author, Conrad de Meester, who argued that Marthe should be rejected as a "false mystic." The main piece of evidence he advanced was his discovery that the descriptions of her visions of Christ's Passion, which she experienced regularly every Friday, were borrowed word for word from preexisting books on the subject. The other members of the commission disagreed with de Meester's negative evaluation, saying that Marthe, who was not a professional writer, may well have used these writings to help her express her own experiences. The commission gave a favorable ruling, and as a result Pope Francis signed a decree officially

revelation given to her by Christ, that the last act of liberty takes place during the interval between clinical death and metaphysical death. This indeed is why the church has prayers for the dying and even for the person who has just expired.

The Struggle of the Last Act of Liberty

The proof that people who have returned from clinical death were not really dead is that they often experienced a spiritual struggle in their coma state, torn between the attraction to the light of love and an opposite temptation to choose the self instead, the hardening of pride that was pushing them towards the darkness. It is this last combat of liberty that Marthe Robin, following the example of Saint Catherine of Siena, carried very specially in her prayer.

The last act of our liberty is so important that it seals our eternal destiny. At that moment, only two possibilities remain: either we die in love, or we die in the rejection of love. It is on this choice that our eternal bliss or eternal damnation will be played out. It is often said that those who die in a state of mortal sin go to hell, but this is only true if they adhere to their mortal sin to the point of making it a veritable sin against the Holy Spirit.

Someone who is in a state of mortal sin has indeed refused the love of God, but he has refused it in one of its consequences expressed by a commandment. The person most probably did not clearly see the intimate connection between this consequence, this "no" by which he opposed the will of God expressed in one of his commandments, and all the love that God has for him. It is not in the context of their everyday lives that most people can really perceive this connection. It would seem that it is only in the ultimate state of a person's life, where the graces of God are extremely strong, that he can really perceive all his acts and see how they

recognizing the "heroicity" of Marthe's virtues in 2014, thus paving the way for her beatification. Conrad de Meester died in 2019, but a book containing his negative evaluation of Marthe as a false mystic was published posthumously, igniting a controversy in France. Rome continues to stand by its proclamation of Marthe's heroicity.

connect with or oppose the love of God. It is only in this way that a person can sum up his entire life, in one last act of liberty, with a "yes" or a "no" to Love itself.

But for this to happen it seems almost indispensable that Love itself be, so to speak, rendered present in person. And I believe that Christ is particularly present to every man at the moment of his death. This is the way I interpret two obscure passages from the First Epistle of Peter in chapter 3, verses 18 to 20, and chapter 4, verse 6. Saint Peter says that after Christ died, he descended into hell. This statement has usually been interpreted as follows: he descended into hell to seek all the righteous who had preceded him in order to introduce them into paradise.

But Saint Peter says something much more mysterious, which the tradition has never really dared take into account. He says that Christ went to announce the Good News to the souls of those who refused to believe in Noah's day, and who perished during the flood. This is extremely obscure and mysterious because one has the impression that Christ preached to and tried to convert the dead, people who had already accomplished their last act of liberty and are therefore fixed in their eternal destiny. On the other hand, we also have the impression that Christ is going to preach to people who have refused to believe and who have therefore condemned themselves, and it is hard to see how Christ could have brought them back by his descent into hell.

I believe that Saint Peter, in this obscure passage of his epistle, is saying that in the mystery of his Passover, Christ, through his grace, meets every person in his or her death. He offers salvation even to people who refused the will of God concerning certain matters during their lives, as was the case with the men of Noah's time. These people were apparently condemned by God in the Bible story, since they perished in the Flood. Everything would therefore lead one to believe that they are damned. But Saint Peter's text reminds us that to every man, regardless of whether or not in his lifetime he knew Christ, regardless of whether he lived before or after Christ, regardless of whether he accepted or refused certain commandments of God during his lifetime, Christ offers salvation at the hour of his death. In this ultimate and mysterious meeting, the love of God is revealed to every man in the same way that it was perceived by the saints who really knew it during their lifetimes. Saint Peter is speaking here about a kind of ultimate, last-minute evangelization: "For this reason the gospel was preached also to those who are dead, that they might be judged according to men in the flesh, but live according to God in the spirit" (1 Pet 4:6 NKJV).

No man is deprived of this encounter with Christ, who died for us all. If it does not happen during a person's lifetime, it at least occurs at the moment of his death. Remember that we are not speaking here of metaphysical death, which definitively seals a person's destiny, but of the moment that precedes it and where each one must still accomplish his last act of liberty.

God Struggles to Tear Us Away from Damnation

It is impossible for us to be damned, to lose forever the love of God, simply because of a certain number of partial refusals of his will for us. It is true that some lives give us a "spine-chilling" impression. The death of Hitler, for example. Or perhaps even more so that of Eichmann, responsible for the extermination of the Jews, who declared during his trial that he would leap for joy in his grave thinking that he had dragged into death six million Jews. One has the impression that such people were already at the very doors of damnation. The possibility of damnation is very real. But the reality of damnation is something so frightful, much more terrible than all the horrors of this world. And for this reason the church absolutely refuses to pronounce on whether or not any given human being is effectively damned. This holds true even for Judas.

The act of damnation itself is essentially a "no" to the love of God, as such; considered in its source and no longer simply through one or the other of God's commandments. Damnation rejoins the sin of Satan. It is an extreme act of demonic pride. It is the "sin against the Holy Spirit." It is no longer a fault of weakness but a sin of pride, for only pride, which is at the root of all sins going back to the original sin, can cause our damnation.

Such a decision supposes that man, whose agony was a mere preparation, is raised up at the moment of death to a state of extremely intense spiritual perception with regard to the mystery of God's love for him and for all men. This does not mean that we can sin as much as we want until the Lord catches up with us with salvation at the last minute. It is obvious that in the course of life, the more one has entered in one way or another into the logic of sin, the more one has descended into the spiral of despair and pride, the more one is on the road to damnation.

But God would not be God, the Father of mercies, who "so loved the world that he gave his only Son" (John 3:16 ESV), if, at the hour of death, the force of divine grace and of the redemptive blood of Jesus did not come to exert its full weight of love precisely on the liberty of a person who has hardened himself and who is leaning towards damnation. Will not this force of grace and redemption manifest itself to him on the face of Christ who died for us on the cross? Will it not be shown to him at the hour of his death in order to elicit the conversion of his heart so that he will be saved? This is perhaps the last-minute evangelization, the final announcement of salvation to the dead about which Saint Peter speaks. This presupposes that the person is given at that moment an extremely acute mystical perception that, however, is not yet the face-to-face vision of God in eternity.

In the case of someone who has already been living in the logic of love, this ultimate experience enables him to fall gently into final salvation like a ripe fruit falling off the tree. But in the case of someone who has during life been caught up in the logic of damnation because of his various mortal sins, this perception causes an absolutely terrible inner spiritual struggle. This is what we can already sense in the agony of some people, and it is likely that the struggle continues after their clinical death. These people are struggling because they do not want to die. Having placed their hope only in this world and its values, they refuse death with all their strength. Even after clinical death, they often have a tense and contracted face for a long time because their soul is still fighting.

The definitive "yes" can sometimes be given before the moment of ascertainable death. For others, it happens after clinical death, when the soul, freed from all bodily perceptions by the brain-death coma but not yet separated metaphysically from the body, sees all its life in the light of God. According to those who have known this state and been revived, the soul perceives its body as from the outside. It is not, strictly speaking, that it is separated from the body, but it is in an exceptional relationship with it, and also in an exceptional relationship with time, similar to the experience described by survivors of automobile accidents who were able to pass in review their entire lives during the few seconds that the accident lasted.

Hope for the Final Conversion of All

It is unthinkable that a God who is the Father of mercy would instantly project into hell young people who, after having amused themselves and perhaps sinned at a party, crashed into a tree and perished while on the way home drunk late at night. Whatever their state in relation to the law of God may have been at that time, and perhaps it was a state of mortal sin, it cannot be that they are just thrown directly into hell without further examination. A damnation of this type is inconceivable, given all that we know about the God of Jesus Christ.

God does not set up traps at places where we come across sharp turns in our lives in order to throw us into hell. Otherwise all sorts of appalling questions would have to be answered: Why did God not give these people time to repent, while to others, who were perhaps more guilty, he gave time, even sending a priest to minster to them before death? On the contrary, we must see God through the parable of the lost sheep, that is to say, as a shepherd who leaves his ninety-nine sheep to run after the hundredth who is lost, so as to bring it back on his shoulders (cf. Luke 15:4–7). "God so loved the world that he gave us his only Son" (John 3:16 ESV). This means that he has set out on a relentless drive to redeem us, right up until the last act of our liberty, and his relentlessness becomes even more intense in the last moments of our life, even if these moments escape clinical observation.

If the opposite were true, the God of whom we speak would not be God, the Father of our Lord Jesus Christ. Indeed, if Christ died on the cross, if he offered his sufferings and his blood to save us, it would be despairing to think that his redemptive work could be so easily defeated. Preachers have always backed away from saying these things, because they believed that if they did say them, people would see it as an encouragement to go on sinning without the fear of God. But I think we have a much stronger desire to obey God and do his will when we know that he is a God who relentlessly persists in working to save us and to "love us to the end." It seems to me that the path of fear is not the most effective way to keep people on the road of obedience to God. I do not think we will be more obedient to a God of whom we are afraid.

The authentic gift of fear consists in being wary of one's own sins, which can lead us to reject God's love. We must put all our hope in God and be distrustful of ourselves, because, precisely, we all have a perception of how we are capable of eternally condemning ourselves by saying "no" to God's love. It is not God who condemns us, it is only we who can condemn ourselves to eternal damnation. But God will strive to save us to the end. Of course, the last word will be said by our liberty, which God cannot force or violate. But we will be besieged at the moment of our death by all the grace coming from Jesus himself and from the communion of saints. This is what many saints have experienced. At the moment of death, the soul will suffer harassment from the demons, with whom it cooperated in this life through sin, but at the same time it will be supported, encouraged, and defended by all the holy souls who have offered their sufferings and trials for the love of God and neighbor. These will now assist the soul in its last spiritual combat.

The final act of our liberty belongs totally to us, but at the same time, if we do not refuse to be loved, it is also entirely given to us by the grace of final perseverance. This is the mystery of grace in our liberty. If we do not say "no," the act of love itself is given to us by God. Our liberty consists in accepting love, consenting to love.

God's relentlessness in accomplishing redemption can win back even those beings who seem entirely filled with darkness. This is why we can and must hope for the salvation even of those beings who have committed the worst abominations. The great Swiss theologian Cardinal Hans Urs von Balthasar has written a book called *Dare We Hope*. I myself believe that we must *hope* for the final conversion of all men. We cannot *believe* with certitude that all are saved, but we must *hope* for it. We would have a very poor idea of the love of God and the greatness of Christ's redemptive sacrifice if we easily accepted the idea that God would have failed to save someone, no matter how far that person had gone along the road of evil. We can of course fear that such and such a person has not been saved, but in that case, it is the refusal on the part of the sinful person that is to be feared. For we must fear ourselves, not God. As Saint Philip Neri once said to God, "O Lord, beware of Philip!" Yes indeed, it is I who can lose myself, but God is the God who saves.

Taking Seriously the Redemptive Sacrifice of Christ

To believe in the God who "loves to the end" is to take seriously the redemptive sacrifice of Christ. If the death of Christ is a failure for some, it should plunge us into the agony that was his in Gethsemane. Jesus said, in a private revelation made to Saint Catherine of Siena, that when he sweated blood at Gethsemane, it was due to those who were destroying in their hearts his redeeming grace. What Jesus lived through then was the "spiritual" combat against sin, a battle in which many saints and holy men and women have participated according to the limited measure of their capacities as finite human creatures. As for Jesus, he accomplished this battle for everyone at Gethsemane. That is where his agony took place. When he was on the cross, he died in great suffering, but it was at Gethsemane that he said, "My soul is very sorrowful, even unto death" (Matt 26:38 ESV); it is there that he experienced great anguish even though his enemies had not yet put their hands on him.

It was there that he accepted the cup, which signifies the entire mystery of our liberty. The blood of Jesus is going to flow into the cup of human liberty, but this cup, if it so chooses, can refuse to receive it. We are the receptacles of God's love, but we can say "no." Jesus experienced this contradiction of our rebellious liberty, but at the same time it was there that he loved us to the end. He sought us in the depths of our perdition in order to pull us out of damnation.

To believe that God can simply resign himself to our damnation is not to believe in the God of the gospel. Human parents worthy of the name would not behave in such a way toward their children, and yet they are still far from the love that is God. If we believe that God is a Father, we must not think that he loves us less than human parents love their children. Of course, God loves us with perfect love, and therefore this love is at the same time perfectly just. But we must trust him! Scripture tells us that God is love. It also tells us that God is just, but it never says that he *is* justice. It is starting from love that divine justice will be accomplished, and not the other way around.

Pursued by the Love of God

The more we head towards damnation, the more we are harassed by the love of God. This is, we have seen, the entire drama of hell. Once we have made the last act of liberty, if it is a "no" that adheres to Satan's "no" of pride, a total "no" to love, then all the love with which God continues to love us, a love in which we are immersed, is transformed by us into a fire that burns us. And it does so endlessly, because God can never stop loving us. It is not possible for God to be the bliss of someone who has become completely refractory to his love. The "outer darkness" (Matt 22:13 ESV) in which the damned enclose themselves is like one of those "black holes" of the universe that do not reflect any light, but destroy whatever light comes to them.

I very much appreciate the most ancient representations of hell found in the icons of the Eastern Church. There it can be noticed that the fire of hell comes directly from God's divine glory that is being contemplated by the blessed. This same glory becomes unbearable for those who refuse it, since their hearts are closed to love. Love tortures them like a fire, and from that moment on they invent in their demonic hatred all sorts of tortures against each other.

Hell is not a torture chamber prepared by God to punish us, nor is it a place outside his love, as if he were to say, "Now that you have said 'no,' it's over, you have fallen exclusively under the regime of my justice. You have withdrawn yourself from my love and therefore I am applying to you my justice in all its rigor." God, being love, can give only love, but it is the damned who accomplish justice. By refusing love, they transform it for themselves into damnation. But God never stops loving them.

Certain saints have gone as far as to pray for the damned, or to offer themselves for them. Saint Thérèse of the Child Jesus said that if she could, she would give her life for the damned. These saints show that they know the heart of God, who cannot stop loving his creatures, even when they are in the state of hell. He continues to love them. It is they and they alone who have the power to make their own damnation.

However, we must not see the ultimate act of our liberty as disconnected from our previous life. This final act is normally prepared by the free acts that preceded it. If we are open to love, our last act of liberty will be like the final words of Saint Thérèse of Lisieux: "O my God, I love you." We will be, as she says of herself, like a cluster of grapes that the Lords picks off the vine. But if we have hardened ourselves, or if we have lived our lives superficially, in frivolity and indifference, our last moments will risk being more traumatic, because we will not be ready.

Likewise, people who die very young and suddenly are usually much less prepared for the final encounter with the Lord than those who pass away at a more mature age, dying a natural death. There are few people who in their youth have already entered into a vision of the meaning of their lives. Most are still caught up in the dizziness and dazzle of discovering the world with its superficial, immediate impressions and the sensual pleasures that it offers.

They are not ready to die. That is why the death of a young person is so shocking. We can accept it only by thinking that Christ was present near him in the last time interval, whose duration eludes us, between clinical death and metaphysical death, and that the person was able to meet the Lord and consent to his love. I do not see why the preparation that God normally gives to those who approach death gradually would not be given by him in a more mysterious way to those who die suddenly.

The Final Consent Given to Love

Sometimes people, no matter how young they may be, make a deliberate gift of their life when they learn that they are close to death. Others make this gift in a less deliberated but equally free manner. I am thinking, for example, of those who jump into the water to rescue someone from drowning, and who perish themselves in the effort to save others. Or those who rush into a burning building in order to save someone and who perish there. In these acts, one freely gives one's life out of love without deliberating. At such moments, the person's liberty is enlightened by the light of the Holy Spirit who shows him that love is the ultimate goal of life.

When someone acts in this way, he responds, even if it be instinctively, to the inspiration of love, and this is the highest form of liberty. Even if everything was played out in one instant, at that moment the person accomplished the most free act he has ever effectuated, because it is an act of perfect charity. Although this act was not rationally deliberated, it was nevertheless desired freely at that critical moment, in a higher way than if it had been deliberated previously. One does not act in this way without wanting to do so from deep down inside oneself. The freest act is not necessarily the one that has been the most carefully thought out and deliberated. The gifts of the Holy Spirit make us perform supremely free acts in a kind of instinctive way, by an inspiration of love. In the cases we are talking about here, the natural instinct that comes into play would, on the contrary, be that of self-preservation: the natural instinct would hardly incite us to throw ourselves into the water or into a fire to save someone else. And we could hardly blame someone for being frightened and having a reflex of self-preservation.

A person who instinctively offers his life as a gift effectuates an act of heroic virtue that is accomplished by an instinct of love inspired by the Holy Spirit. This is something entirely beyond immediate deliberation: the person does not weigh the pros and cons, he acts simply out of love, and this act of love carries everything.

The final act of our liberty at the moment of death is probably of the same order: we simply consent to love. That is why it is very important to place a crucifix in front of a person who is dying, especially if he can no longer speak. Often the last act of liberty can no longer be expressed by words, but is made by a touch, a kiss, a look, or a bodily expression.

6

Entering Heaven

To Die in Perfect Love

THE LAST ACT OF our liberty consists in accepting that God is love, that the principle of creation is love, and that the ultimate goal or end of everything, including our life, is a mystery of love. This act of love is accessible through the grace of Christ to every man without exception, since Jesus shed his blood for all without exception. This consent to love can, for some, be an act of perfect charity, and in this case the soul throws itself directly into God's arms and is immediately introduced into heaven. For others, this consent may still be mixed with elements of egoistic and selfish love—not, however, to the point where it causes them to reject charity, but enough so that it tarnishes the fire of God's love in their hearts. In this case, the soul must go through what the church calls purgatory. As for hell, my experience in accompanying the dying has shown me that the final hardening of the soul in the rejection of love is certainly a possibility. It is indeed a very formidable risk. But, at the same time, among the people I accompanied, I think it highly unlikely that such a thing ever actually took place.

I would go even further. My deep conviction is that a great many people go directly to heaven. There are of course many more saints than those who are officially canonized: there are all those who are in heaven after having gone through the purification of purgatory, but also many saints who have gone directly from the earth to heaven, many more than those found in the martyrology and the church calendar. These are the multitudes celebrated on All Saints' Day. For many, purgatory is already accomplished here on earth, especially through the patiently loving acceptance of the small and great sufferings of life. These, when offered in love, have a purifying effect. There is also the passive purification of illness and agony, which is a real purgatory. To make the offering of one's life in love, as many do when they are dying, is in all likelihood an act of perfect charity.

Plenary Indulgence at the Moment of Death

Finally, we find the mystery of the communion of saints. As I have said, the priestly ministry that I have always accomplished with the greatest joy is the recommendation of the soul of a dying person: it is very moving to be able in this way to place a person in the hands of God. Unfortunately, priests are only rarely requested for this ministry. It is very important, as we have seen, that someone's agony take place in a prayerful environment and that people not wait until the patient is already in a coma before calling a priest. It is far better that the soul's recommendation to God take place while the patient is still conscious, so that he himself can present the offering of his life. Let us recall what was said earlier: this recommendation of the soul must not be confused with the sacrament of the sick, which is, first of all, an anointing of the sick person with the Spirit of strength in view of healing him. This sacrament was in the past almost always referred to as "extreme unction" or the "last sacrament" and it became automatically and almost exclusively linked to the final prayers for the recommendation of the soul. However, the truly "last sacrament" normally intended to accompany the recommendation of the soul and the prayers for the dying is the Eucharist in the form of the viaticum. In the recommendation of the soul, before the actual recommendation, there is a very important act of the church called the plenary indulgence, which is linked, as we have seen, to the mystery of the communion of saints. This mystery works in such a way that, through what theology calls the "reversibility of merits," and based on what Saint Paul says about how we neither live nor die for ourselves alone (cf. Rom 14:7), all the offerings made in love by members of Christ's mystical body can become, through the ministry of the church, a plenary indulgence for someone else. This person will receive as a present, as a gift, the purification that has been earned for him by the sufferings of Christ as well as by those of his brothers and sisters in Christ.

When a priest gives this plenary indulgence, we know with the certitude of faith that the person who receives it (supposing, of course, that he has ultimately consented in his heart to God's love) goes directly to heaven as soon as he dies (without having to undergo in purgatory any purification that his past sins may have merited for him). Some might find such a thing unfair. But I have personally seen that the justice of God is nevertheless fully satisfied in these instances. I would not say that these people suffer more than others, but in general, following the reception of this plenary indulgence, they seem to make of their death a particularly intense gift of themselves in love. My impression is that, in their own way, they are at that moment inspired to offer themselves in turn for others in the communion of the saints.

Christ gave to his apostles the power to bind and unbind on earth. God himself is "bound" by the plenary indulgence of the church, in the sense that when it is given, God grants this grace through the ministry of the priest. But in other cases (when access to a priest is not possible), God is free to give the plenary indulgence without going through the ministerial act of the church. He himself can simply introduce the soul into the state of perfect charity, which is a state "of love for God and the neighbor," a love "that goes unto folly," to quote a beautiful expression coined by Jacques Maritain. This "folly or madness" consists in the fact that the state of perfect charity inspires one to love God and the neighbor not only *as* oneself but *more* than oneself.

The Love of God unto Folly Is Already Heaven

Love unto folly is a love that gives itself totally without waiting for anything in return. Persons who love in this way are completely carried away by the momentum of self-giving. One can only enter paradise when one dwells in this perfect love, and if there are some who must go through purgatory first, it is because when they died, love was not yet perfect in them to this degree. The Lord, however, enables many human beings to enter directly into heaven, fully consummated in this perfect love through the mystery of the communion of saints and through the purifications of the last moments of their life in this world. I have noticed how the eyes of many gravely ill patients often manifest a great and total surrender to love. One can already perceive on their faces the light of God's kingdom.

That is why I do not doubt that there are many people who die in a state of perfect love and go directly to heaven, even if they were not saints during their lives. Jacques Maritain says this very well in a passage from a book that appeared after his death and which is entitled *Untrammeled Approaches*. The work is made up of the interviews that Maritain gave during the last period of his life after the death of his wife, Raïssa, to the Little Brothers of Jesus, a congregation of which he finally became a member and that was founded by the spiritual sons of Charles de Foucauld. Maritain, who had arrived at a very advanced age (he was between eighty and ninety years old), transmitted here his deepest, most profound thought. In what follows, we will be borrowing from the chapter of the book entitled "The Moment of Death," which is part of the interview on "Love and Friendship."

Today You Will Be with Me in Paradise

"What about the preparation or predisposing of a soul in relation to the moment of death?" This is how Jacques Maritain begins. He then enumerates the four cases where a soul goes directly to heaven upon dying.

First case: "The first case is that of a soul who, after having entered the mystical life or the regime of the love of God unto folly, has reached the end of its journey and has achieved as far as it is possible here below, purely and simply and in all respects, the perfection of love. Such a soul is prepared and ready not only to be saved by perhaps passing through purgatory, but also to be united with Jesus in heaven as soon as it leaves the body. If, therefore, the soul perseveres in these dispositions and crosses the threshold of death in a perfect act of the love of God unto folly, it goes straight to heaven." It is clear that Maritain is talking here about a saint, a person who, regardless of whether or not he has been officially canonized, has, in this life, completely followed through on the demands of love until the end, and has reached, according to the measure of his capacities, the perfection of charity. There are many saints of this caliber who may have lived their lives unnoticed by others, simply because they were not surrounded by a religious community that could record the testimony of their exceptional holiness and have it recognized by the church. This is often the case for a good many laypeople. But most of the time, saints who have for a greater part of their lives been animated and inflamed by a love of God unto folly are noticed at least by their loved ones and are said to die in the "odor of sanctity." Although these people have not been officially canonized or "raised to the altars" by the church, they are nonetheless the object of a sort of spontaneous and private veneration on the part of all who knew them.

Second case: "This is the case of a soul who has remained under the regime of friendship with God and who, although it has not yet entered into the mystical state, has come to the end of its journey and has reached here the perfection of love in certain respects (in terms of intensity but not yet with regard to the ability of the soul to be totally dispossessed of itself). This soul is prepared and ready not only to be saved by, perhaps, passing through purgatory, but to join (to be united to) Jesus at the very moment when it leaves its body. If it perseveres in these dispositions, the moment of death will also be the moment when the love of God unto folly declares itself to be that soul's sovereign ruler, so that it can, in a perfect act of love for God unto folly, cross the threshold of death and go straight to heaven." Here we touch upon the mystery of the surplus of grace, which is given by God at the moment of death. A soul who has experienced a great friendship with God, and therefore a very perfect form of love, but who has not achieved the total gift of self which essentially constitutes holiness or sainthood, is entirely prepared and ready to be introduced by God into the state of love unto folly at the moment of death. Because we must not forget that perfect charity is the only door through which we can enter heaven, since heaven is the place where God is loved unto folly and where human beings and angels love him in this "mad" love.

Third case: "The third case is that of a soul who possesses love but who has not yet achieved the perfection of charity (neither absolutely speaking, nor even in regard to certain of its aspects). This soul is prepared and ready to be saved by passing, perhaps, through purgatory, but not to join (be united to) Jesus at the very moment when it leaves the body. Nevertheless, we know that such a soul, if it passes through the moment of death in a perfect act of charity (which can only be an act of love for God unto folly), will be able to enter heaven immediately and be united to Jesus." Here we have the mystery of the moment of death: even a certain share of imperfection in the love of a soul who is in a state of grace cannot stand in the way of the Lord, if he chooses to plunge that soul immediately into an act of love unto folly for himself.

Fourth case: "Finally, the fourth case is that of a soul who does not have charity but lives in evil and who is neither prepared nor ready to be saved or to join (be united to) Jesus at the moment when it leaves its body. However, we know that in a supreme surge of charity it can be saved at this last moment, and furthermore, it can join (be united to) Jesus immediately. 'Today you will be with me in paradise' [Luke 23:42 ESV]."

Here we have a supreme lesson concerning the strength of God's redeeming love: the Good Thief, who was probably not in a state of grace, and was therefore ready neither to be saved nor to be united to Jesus the moment he left his body, was in fact not only united to him, but immediately united to him. Together with Jesus, he entered directly into paradise, going ahead of all the righteous whom Jesus subsequently delivered by his descent into hell on Holy Saturday. This sinner, who was not prepared, was nonetheless introduced by God at the moment of his death into the regime of love for him unto folly. Suddenly, in a flash, he was placed on a level equivalent to that of the greatest mystical saints, the level of Saint Francis of Assisi when he received the stigmata, or of Saint Teresa of Ávila when she was transfixed with divine love . . .

The Particular Judgment

The four scenarios presented by Jacques Maritain show us that we are saved by consenting to the love with which God loves us. This is a far cry from certain sculptural representations, which have nothing Christian about them, even though we find them on the porches of many cathedrals. These representations depict a weighing of souls. They show an angel holding a scale on which a soul's good deeds are placed on one side and its sins on the other. If the scale tips towards the side of the good deeds, the soul goes to heaven, and if it tips in the other direction, the soul goes to hell! Nothing like this is found in divine revelation. The theme of the weighing of souls actually comes from ancient Egypt; from there it passed into certain Christian traditions, which are not those of the best quality.

Our salvation is decided by the consent of our liberty to the saving love of God. This consent can only be given in an act of extreme humility. We must welcome salvation by being aware of our immense poverty, our total indignity in relation to the love of God. The only thing that can really damn us is pride. Even if our faults were as high as the walls of a fortress, the grace of God could knock them down as if with one single blow of a ram, if they only were not cemented by pride. To die outside of love implies not only that one does not love, but, above all, that one refuses to be loved. That is the supreme act of pride and damnation. Whenever we do not accept being loved out of pride, we are already advancing a little further on the road to hell. Pride is the matrix of sin: it alone can cause us to sin against the Holy Spirit.

That which theology designates as the "particular judgment" and which immediately follows death concerns a person's last act of liberty. Was it an act of love for God unto folly? If so, this act in itself introduces the soul into paradise. It does not necessarily have to be something extraordinary. A person who has become all patience and all forgiveness, as was the case with many of the dying patients to whom I ministered, a person who has entirely offered and surrendered himself is already in the state of love unto folly, because he gives himself without waiting for anything in return, except for God who is love itself. This person is in the process of completely offering himself up; he is, therefore, in a certain sense, already in paradise. The particular judgment will simply reveal the reality of the kingdom that was already dwelling in him.

The person who dies in love, but whose soul has not reached the perfection of charity, plunges spontaneously and joyfully into purgatory. His desire is that the love that he already possesses will soon be able to shine incandescently as love unto folly. In order for this to happen, he asks only to be cleansed from the blemishes in his heart resulting from his sin. He also wants to offer for others the suffering he is enduring due to love: these are the blessed sufferings of purgatory that we will discuss later.

The last case is that of the final hardening of the soul against love. This is frightening and dreadful because it is possible, but it is something from which we hope, with all our hope in the redemption, that the blood of Jesus Christ has preserved all human beings.

Heaven or the Supreme Liberty of Love

Heaven is the place where one is supremely free. When I affirm this, it can come across as a provocation because people often answer me by saying, "How can you say that in heaven we are free, since we will no longer be able to choose evil?" To which I reply: "Your idea of liberty is a strange one indeed if you believe that it is characterized, as such, by the capacity to choose evil!" The fruit of liberty is love. Liberty in a soul that is not yet consummated in love, but which here below is still on the road to perfect love, necessarily has the capacity to sin. To prevent the risk of sin, it would be necessary to suppress liberty, but doing so would prevent it from bearing its normal fruit, which is love. This, in turn, would prevent the soul from reaching its ultimate destination, the goal for which it was created. God does not want this. But once liberty has arrived at the perfection of love unto folly, once the soul has freely chosen perfect charity and entered the kingdom of heaven, it cannot turn back. From then on, the soul is not only perfectly free in not sinning, but it is precisely because its liberty has reached perfection that it does not sin.

In what does this liberty of heaven consist? Many Christians think of heaven as a kind of dormitory. This is due to the fact that it is often said of a deceased person that he has "fallen asleep in the Lord." This very ancient expression is already found in Saint Paul. It means that the body has "fallen asleep" and is awaiting the resurrection. But the soul has not fallen asleep at all. To prove this, it is enough to open the book of Revelation to the sixth chapter and see how the souls of the martyrs, under the altar of heaven, intercede for their brothers and sisters who remain on earth (Rev 6:9–11). The Epistle to the Hebrews also says that we have approached "the spirits of the righteous [who have] been made perfect" (Heb 12:23 ESV). Heaven is thus a place of intense spiritual activity.

Unfortunately, because of sin, we believe that liberty consists in being the primary cause of our acts, but this is not true. We are the primary cause of our actions only when we do evil. When we do good, we are always the secondary cause, because it is God who is the primary source of our good deeds (cf. Eph 2:10). In heaven all our acts will be a response to the divine initiative. This is why the life of heaven is a liturgy.

That does not mean that in heaven they do nothing but organize processions and sing hymns. We must not think that the heavenly liturgy is in the image of our earthly liturgies. On the contrary, it is our earthly liturgies that are only a rather distant image of the heavenly liturgy. The latter is a liturgy of love, because all the initiatives of the saints in heaven flow from the heart of God. They are echoes of the desire of his heart, a desire that is refracted in the diversity of the members of the body of Christ. To every desire of God's heart corresponds a spiritual creature, an angel or a man. Each one of these echoes and expresses a desire of God, not by a kind of mechanical reproduction but by his liberty, as the living instrument of God's will.

We see this in the book of Revelation: there is a constant coming and going of angels; the souls of the righteous shout and beseech; there is an extraordinary spiritual activity. It is like a huge fireworks display of love, involving much more than the simple one-to-one relationship of each person with God. We must not think of the beatific vision as an immense flash of divine light that leaves everyone dazzled, saturated with happiness, but so dazed that they are no longer able to look at anyone else. This extremely depleted conception of the beatific vision is almost similar to the representation of heaven as a dormitory.

Instead, we ought to think of the beatific vision as a kind of circulation of love, starting from the Trinity, which is its heart, and flowing through all human and angelic beings. Therefore, all the blessed inhabitants of heaven, through their love of God, also love each other. And as long as the history of the world is not completed, those in heaven also love those on earth as well as those in purgatory.

I also think they must even love those who are in hell, the fallen angels certainly, and humans, if any there be who are damned. The saints love the damned inasmuch as they are creatures of God. Indeed, heaven is nothing but love, and love remains love, even when it is scorned and rejected. The revolt of Satan gave rise to the mystery of God's scorned love. Léon Bloy, and after him, Jacques and Raïssa Maritain, were deeply moved by this thought when they reflected on the tears shed by the Blessed Virgin during her apparition at La Salette. All this indicates that the happiness of heaven is not merely an earthly felicity, but that it is the fullness of love, even when this love is scorned by those who reject it. Heaven is the place of bliss because it is the place of love. But the beatitude of love unto folly can also involve the wound of love that has been trampled and scorned, as is illustrated by the stigmata of the risen Christ. The bliss of heaven can assume this wound in a love that does not cease to be love, even without experiencing any suffering in the human sense as a lack or deprivation of happiness, since love in heaven is perfect.

The Intercession of Heaven

The mystery remains, but it is certain that in heaven the angels and saints are intensely involved in all that is happening on earth and that there is, as Jesus says, "more joy in heaven over one sinner who repents than over ninety-nine righteous persons who need no repentance" (Luke 15:7 ESV).

The mystery involving the humiliation and suffering of innocent children and the persecution of the righteous, the mystery of those who live according to the beatitudes, assumed in love, even when that love is scorned and rejected: all this is also present in heaven. It will continue to be there as long as the history of the redemption lasts, and even beyond, in relation to the definitive rejection of love by those who are in hell. Heaven is a state that we can hardly imagine, because those who are there have already reached the goal: they stand before God in possession of love. But at the same time, as long as human history is not over, the communion or fellowship of the heavenly church with that of the earth and with that of purgatory causes heaven to participate intensely in our life, in our journey, in our sanctification.

In Jacques Maritain's book *Untrammeled Approaches*, which we have already mentioned, there is another chapter, entitled

"About the Church of Heaven," in which the author gives advice about how to address our requests to heaven. When we pray to heaven for an intention, instead of entrusting a request formulated in advance to our favorite saint, Maritain suggests doing the opposite. Faced with a particular situation, one should ask oneself which saint, during his life, needed to deal with something analogous. Then we should ask him to intercede, but not by saying, "I ask you for this or that," but instead, "You who see God, you who see all things in God, please ask for whatever is most important and most necessary for me, and I shall remain united with you in your prayer."

Without knowing it, Maritain echoed here one of the methods of prayer used by Saint Ignatius of Loyola. The latter, before entering into prayer, asked God to discern to which saint he should pray. The prayer of Saint Ignatius was that of a man of action who was at the same time a very great contemplative. At the end of his life, having become the General of the Society of Jesus, he prayed seven hours a day. His prayer was very much action oriented because he carried in his heart the mission of the church and the nascent Society of Jesus in view of the evangelization of the world.

Because he had to carry this heavy burden made up of the cares of the church, he would ask the Lord, whenever a particular concern arose, to make him discern the saint to whom he should pray about it. He basically felt that his prayer was only valuable if it flowed into the intentions of the saints in heaven. The prayer of petition or supplication is a very beautiful thing, but there comes a time when we realize that those who can best intercede for us before the Lord are the saints. Not only the canonized saints, but also holy men and women whom we have known and who have died in the friendship of God.

The souls in purgatory can also intercede for us. They cannot merit for themselves, but they offer for others their sufferings out of a love that is engaged in making reparations. We can, of course, pray for these souls and assist them in their purification, but they can help us even more, because they see our problems in the light of God.

As for the saints in heaven, they see us as God sees us, and so they are able to clearly discern what we need. This is a very profound aspect of Saint Ignatius's prayer method. Not that one must always pray in this way, but this abandonment to the communion of saints is extremely helpful in times of distress and spiritual dryness. It suffices to say, "I kneel beside you, Blessed Virgin Mary, or you, Saint Thérèse of Lisieux." I can then enter into the prayer of the saint next to whom I have placed myself; there is now no need for me to formulate the prayer myself. The saint I have chosen is doing it infinitely better than I in heaven. I can simply pour myself into the intercession of this saint who expresses a desire of the heart of God according to his personality, according to his psychology, according to his history, according to the image of his saintliness.

We can also pray by making ours the prayer of Christians who are still alive. We are often asked to pray for the intentions of the Holy Father or our bishop. Although they are not yet saints, they are Christians who carry very heavy burdens in their ministry, and who are faced with many of the distresses of the church that we do not know. They count very much on us to pray for their intentions. Although we may not know what these intentions are, we can entrust them to God in faith. In a similar manner, I can ask the Lord to fulfill all the good wishes that he puts in the hearts of my brothers and sisters.

Friendship with the Saints of Heaven

Friendship with the saints of heaven and with the dead, whom we believe to be in heaven or purgatory, is something indispensable to our life of faith. As we grow older, we have more and more loved ones who have already entered eternity. It is very important to give them time. The time we devote to God must also be a time when we find them in him. There is nothing that weighs down our heart more than the disappearance of a loved one in a daily life that continues on its course. It is as if suddenly a hatch has engulfed him, severing him from the course of our occupations and our daily worries. We fully realize that we have lost a friend when we have to erase his name and number from our list of phone contacts. It may seem ridiculous, but when we lose someone we love, what often hurts us the most is to have to make the last banal gestures that exclude him from our lives: disposing of his clothes, closing up his apartment . . . How would it be possible not to look for him then alongside the Lord? It is absolutely not a question of evoking the dead by magical means, but rather of invoking them in the Lord. We should call out to them in the communion that puts us together with them in an attitude of adoration before God, the Blessed Trinity. We can invoke their help and their presence in our journey towards God.

I believe that God sometimes allows the deceased to briefly twinkle at us, giving us little signs of their presence. In this area, each one has his secrets. But departed souls have very delicate, very subtle ways of showing us that they are alive with God, that they are close to us and that they take a keen interest in our lives. Since God our Father is all love, and since he is fully engaged with his Son and with his Spirit in the work of our redemption, how could the souls of heaven not be interested and concerned about our salvation? In heaven, what do they discuss if not our salvation and our entire human adventure? All our history unfolds in the heart of God, in the heart of the Trinity. Our history is our love, our refusal of love, the opening or the closing of our hearts. Heaven is the place from which go forth towards us innumerable initiatives of love. Thérèse the Little Flower said before dying, "I want to spend my heaven doing good on the earth." For this word alone, she rightly deserves to be proclaimed a Doctor of the Church, because it is a word that has never been said and that is nevertheless a fundamental truth.

Heaven after the Resurrection of the Flesh

After the resurrection, when history will be no more, when redemption will have been completed, what will happen in heaven? Will boredom reign? No, not in the least, because love is always imaginative. If we have not understood this, it's because we have not really learned to love, even in the human sense of the word.

Lovers do not get bored; creativity is an essential trait of love. Love constantly creates and re-creates. When God makes "all things new" out of love, it will in no way be an inert creation.

Here we can use the term *heavenly liturgy* in the sense that it will be like a choir or orchestra in which there are various instruments and where each player retains his particularity. Unlike a regular orchestra, we will not play a melody written in advance; it will be more like a jazz orchestra where the melody is constantly invented by the musicians. This will express an extraordinary communion, a permanent invention.

The heavenly liturgy will be like a display of fireworks made up of all the different expressions of human holiness, bearing the trace of history through time and in the various races, languages, and nations. Everyone will express themselves together in communion, composing a kind of immense memorial of human history. God loves our history. This history, which sometimes seems so mediocre to us, will be transfigured and entirely assumed by love; it will be the very substance of the heavenly liturgy. Jacques Maritain likes to say that the angels will relate history to us. We humans are witnesses of only a very small part of history, the part that we have contributed to make; but history is also that of the cosmos, before man was created. Indeed, there are a great many things that man has lived through as if he were half asleep. This is true even of events from our own lives. In heaven, we shall look back on our lives in a way that will seem extraordinary.

We will see all the graces that flowed from the communion of the saints, for events that were apparently banal but where the destiny of our salvation was finally played out. To see this, we will need the help of the angels, whose keen x-ray-like perceptions will reveal to us the full depth and scope of the work of grace in the smallest aspects of human existence. This will inspire us all, in a resonance of love among ourselves, to send up to the throne of God a concert of praise.

This is the scene depicted by Fra Angelico's magnificent painting, *The Resurrection of the Dead*. In it, we see on the left the elect who enter paradise, where they are met by angels and saints who invite them to dance together with them in a circle. Angels and men hold hands, embrace, and hug each other as they dance towards the heavenly Jerusalem, which is seen in a radiant corner of the picture.

Isn't this exactly what we request in the recommendation of the soul at the moment of death, when during the litany of the saints we ask the angels and the saints to come and seek the soul and accompany it to paradise? We invite Christ himself, of course, but also, along with him, the Blessed Virgin Mary, Saint Joseph, patron of the good death, our guardian angel and our patron saint, as well as those saints whom we have most loved and prayed to during our life.

In Universal Communion

One last aspect of the communion of the saints in heaven is that it is universal. We will enter heaven in total communion with men of all races, languages, epochs, and nations. Saint John speaks in the book of Revelation of a "great multitude that no one could number" (Rev 7:9 ESV) and whose singing is "like the roar of many waters" (Rev 14:2 ESV). This might almost seem frightening. We are going to meet Adam and all his descendants. Our hearts will have to expand far beyond the relationships we have had on this earth. But it is clear that we could not dwell in God's love unto folly if there was even one person next to whom we did not want to be in heaven. A desire to exclude someone else from heaven would be a definite sign of damnation.

However, this vast host of heaven will not be something inorganic, a crowd of individuals juxtaposed one next to the other, because it is the body of Christ and, consequently, each member is attached to the whole by other members. The little finger is attached to the arm by the bones of the hand. This means that beings who have been given to us here below are meant to be our closest companions in eternity. It is in paradise, in the communion of the saints, that the reality of friendship will exist to the highest degree, no longer involving exclusions of any kind, and free of all that which, in a friendship on the earth, may have been imperfect.

We will have then, as we already do in this life on our spiritual journey, companions of eternity who will be like the binding agents of our insertion into the universal communion, creating the meshes by which God attaches us to it. These are the people God has placed closest to us, so that we love them first on this earth. Our parents, by whom he gave us life, and then the friends who are our brothers in the Spirit. We can be sure that what begins between us here, if it is really the work of charity, will continue in heaven. We enter as of now into the reality of an eternal companionship.

That is also why, starting in this life, there are certain saints, certain angels, to whom we are more particularly entrusted. Hence the importance of choosing the name of a child at baptism. To give a name to a child is to entrust it especially to the patronage of a saint or an angel. Then come the saints whom we ourselves have chosen, because among the saints we have certain friends whom we love with predilection. And if we love them in this way, it is because they themselves have chosen us first, because they are our elders and our love is an answer to their initiative of love. God takes pleasure in all this because his universality is not a flat uniformity; he wants the heavenly Jerusalem to be made with precious stones of different colors (cf. Rev 21:19–20). In heaven, all the spiritual families will shine out through all the various forms of holiness. We will not be lost in an anonymous crowd, but integrated into an organic communion, the body of the risen Christ.

We will also discover that we are linked to Christ's body by those who gave their lives for us, as well as by those for whom we gave our lives. We will then discover some for whom we gave our life without even knowing them, because God and the church freely dispose of the offering we make of ourselves. And thus we will be surprised to see grateful brothers coming to us, people whom we have not even chosen, but who will have been chosen by God for us, because we will have suffered for them for the sake of Jesus, and Jesus and his church will have disposed of this love for their salvation. We will discover on our side unknown benefactors who have been for us invisible channels of grace. The world of the kingdom is an infinitely personalized one, a "city that is bound firmly together" (Ps 122:3 ESV), where everything is connected because each one leans on his neighbor in the love of Christ.

7

Purgatory

The Requirement That Love Be Purified

DIRECT ENTRY INTO HEAVEN after death is the most normal access to eternal life. We do not know if it is the most frequent one. If we spontaneously tend to doubt this, it is probably because we do not have enough confidence in the love of God for us. Maybe it's because we fail to see sufficiently that God not only forgives us and erases our sins, but that he is able to sanctify us "to the end," and that he is capable of bringing us directly to heaven in the fullness of his love, thanks to the concentration of graces that occurs in the last moments of life. Perhaps we would realize this better if we had more experience accompanying the dying.

The fact that even a great sinner like the Good Thief was able to enter paradise directly without going through purgatory should not shock us, but give us instead the desire to experience already, in this life, a total conversion to eternal life. We can, as we have seen, already have in this life foretastes of purgatory, moments when we endure hardships in a spirit of love and where we are purified by this love.

Unfortunately, we are often forgetful of the great pressure of love that God exerts in our hearts by his grace. This is why we spontaneously feel that we are not ready to see the God who is love face-to-face. I think this presentiment is at the root of the theory of reincarnation. It is a doctrine as old as the world. It claims that to be totally purified, man needs to go through many lives. He cannot cover in one single life the immense distance that separates him from God. He would supposedly need to return several times, each time to a different body in order to begin another life. Perhaps in our Catholic circles we have not spoken enough about purgatory lately. Asking oneself if one is truly ready to enter the love of God is an authentic question for the human spirit. Without having necessarily done much evil, we have not always allowed ourselves to be inflamed by the love of God.

We will now examine the doctrine of purgatory, recalling the teaching of the Catholic faith on this point, and how it developed in the church. We will try above all to understand what purgatory really is. Some of what used to be said about purgatory has been very detrimental to the authentic doctrine itself, and that is one of the reasons it is almost never taught or preached anymore today by priests. Nonetheless in the eyes of the church it is a revealed truth, a dogma of faith. Purgatory was often misrepresented to the point of travesty, and when a mystery has been presented in a distorted manner, it becomes impossible, sooner or later, to mention it at all. Something similar happened with the doctrine concerning angels: at one point, people ceased talking about the subject, because it had been represented too simplistically in the past. But, in getting rid of imperfect imagery, they ended up discarding an authentically revealed reality.

How Is Purgatory Revealed to Us?

How do we know that there is a purgatory? We have no direct revelation of it in the Word of God, as we do concerning heaven and hell. The Protestant reformers of the sixteenth century, wishing to return to Scripture alone, felt that it was their duty to eliminate the doctrine of purgatory as if it were an outgrowth invented by men. In actual fact, the reality is much more complex.

We know that at the end of the period when the history of Israel in the Old Testament is concluded, that is, less than two centuries before the coming of Christ, the Jews believed in and practiced prayers for the dead. Faith in purgatory was to be developed from faith in the usefulness of these prayers, from the Jewish belief that the sacrifices offered for the dead can purify them of some of their faults. This is attested to by the Second Book of the Maccabees in chapter 12, verse 45. After a battle, Judas Maccabeus learned that some of the dead bodies of Jewish soldiers had been found with amulets of idols. These men were infected with idolatry, yet they died fighting for the faith of the God of Israel. They had died as martyrs but at the same time they were not exempt from superstition. Even today there are sincere Christians who, more or less unconsciously, remain superstitious.

Judas Maccabeus therefore ordered that an atoning sacrifice be offered for these men who had probably died in the friendship of God, since they had given their lives for him, but who, nonetheless, were tainted with idolatrous impurity. The text praises Judas for doing this, saying, "it was a holy and pious thought" (2 Macc 12:45 RSVCE). This gesture was therefore truly inspired by God, and it shows that already, before Christ, the faith of Israel conceived that there could be some purification of the soul beyond death.

This is what is called purgatory. Prayers for the dead imply the existence of a state of purification after death. It does not make sense to pray for a dead person if you do not believe in the existence of purgatory. The Protestants are therefore perfectly coherent when they do not pray for the dead, because they believe that they have immediately entered into their final state, and that there is no longer any reason to ask that they be purified. But from the times of the early church, we see the development of prayers for the dead. The prayer asking that the dead may "rest in peace" left traces even in the inscriptions of the catacombs. These prayers sometimes take the form of wishes addressed directly to the departed person: "May you rest in peace! May you live forever!" and others of the sort.

This phenomenon developed gradually in the life of the church. Towards the tenth century AD, the monastery of Cluny introduced the feast of the commemoration of all the faithful departed, on the day following the Solemnity of All the Saints. The first of November celebrates all the faithful who have entered the glory of heaven. With the authorization of the church, the monks of Cluny devoted the following day to prayers for the departed faithful who have not yet entered the glory of God: the souls of purgatory.

These two liturgical days have become somewhat mingled in the practice of the faithful in France and elsewhere. Very often families will pray for their deceased at the cemetery on November 1, because that day is a public holiday. In fact, liturgically, there are two separate celebrations. The first, that of All Saints on November 1, celebrates in joy the triumph of all the saved who are in glory. The second, that of November 2, intercedes for the faithful who still need to be cleansed before entering the clear vision of God. The church, in establishing these celebrations, showed that it was aware of the implications of Israel's faith and liturgy. Moreover, the Jews today continue to pray for the dead.

In the Eastern churches, the development of the faith in purgatory is confined simply to the practice of prayers for the dead. These churches never felt the need to make things any more explicit. In the West, two ecumenical councils—the Council of Florence in the fifteenth century and the Council of Trent, which in the sixteenth century addressed the denials of Luther and Calvin on this point—were led to dogmatically define the existence of purgatory. They did so, however, with extreme caution, offering no descriptions, in order to leave open for theologians the question of *how* this purification takes place.

In particular, the magisterium of the church has always avoided speaking of the "fire" of purgatory, even though this word has come up in the writings of certain theologians and has been used in preaching. This word unfortunately created a false connection between purgatory and hell. With regard to the latter, Scripture does sometimes speak of a "fire." This connection gave rise to a certain imagery that resulted in a distorted presentation of purgatory that was somewhat of a caricature.

Purgatory Is Not a Hell of Limited Duration

Purgatory has sometimes been described as a temporary hell. According to this faulty presentation, those who are damned go to hell forever, while those who are not, but who are not directly admitted to the vision of God, are sent to a place very much like hell where they are punished by fire, but only for a limited time. One day they will come out purified and go to heaven.

We know that this presentation is incorrect, even when it comes to hell. Let us reiterate tirelessly that it is not God who makes hell. God is love and he can only love his creatures. The same love that for the blessed is supreme happiness becomes for the souls in purgatory the source of a purifying type of suffering, and for the damned, a fire that consumes and tortures. The same gift of God's love causes, according to the disposition in which each person receives it, either the bliss of heaven, the purifying suffering of purgatory, or the despairing pain of hell.

Purgatory: The Grace of Reparation through Love

Purgatory exists for souls who, at the moment of death, find themselves in the presence of God's love and discover that, although they have not refused it, they have ignored it most of the time. They have even often mistreated it during their lifetime, without having directly rejected it. They are saved and therefore they could enter heaven. But along with love, the truth is also given to them. Love and truth go hand in hand. Love brings to light the truth of our life with all its acts. It is what we have referred to as the "particular judgment."

At that moment, we see what our life has been in the light of God. We see not only our bad deeds, but also how poorly we have responded to the love with which God loves us. In addition, we measure the extent to which, due to our evil deeds and sins of omission, the Lord's loving redemptive plan has been deprived of graces that he intended for others in the communion of saints. We see how others, starting with those closest to us, have suffered from the unfortunate consequences of our lack of love and generosity.

In moments of true repentance, we realize the harm we have done to others and we suffer to the point of being brokenhearted. The suffering of repentance is something blessed. It has nothing to do with remorse or guilt. Remorse only causes us to turn in on ourselves. It is remorse that led Judas to commit suicide. We do not know if immediately thereafter, in the last moment of his life, he made an act of true repentance. Repentance liberates us from self-centeredness and self-defeating guilt. It turns us towards God and towards others, showing us how much we have hurt them. We come to regret our sin because we are dwelling in love, and repentance is the fruit of love.

There is not the least shadow of repentance in hell, since it consists in the rejection of love itself. We must not think of hell as a human tribunal where a person, after being sentenced to death, breaks down saying, "If only I could start my life over again, I would act differently!" A person cannot go to hell if he is in this state. One goes to hell only in a state of hardening, that is to say, in a state of pride. The soul is in pride when it does not repent because it neither loves nor wants to be loved; it prefers its own ego, confinement within itself, rather than the communion of love.

Perfect love takes us directly to heaven, because at the moment of death, the act of perfect charity superabundantly compensates all the faults that we may have committed. The Good Thief had many sins and perhaps even some ghastly crimes on his conscience, and at the time of the particular judgment he saw all of these. But the act of perfect charity which he made while suffering next to Jesus on the cross superabundantly compensated for everything. He made amends for everything in his simple act of faith and of love for Jesus. The wounds that he had inflicted on the communion of saints were also superabundantly compensated. For merit is nothing other than the fruit of charity. And charity is the fecundation of grace and of faith.

The person who dies in love without being in perfect charity, with a heart full of immediate worries because he has not yet totally invested himself in the love of God and neighbor, is still very much imbued with selfishness. But, as we had said, he will find himself in the presence of the love with which God has loved him throughout his life. Simultaneously, he will see all his refusals of grace, which have not been absolute—otherwise they would have led to damnation—but which may still have been quite serious, either through omission, by action, by word, or by thought. For the most part, he was aware of these sins, he repented of them and confessed them. But he did not fully satisfy the demands of love, he did not make amends for the harm that he caused not only by offending the love of God, but by wounding the communion of saints.

Offering the Suffering of Love for the Salvation of Others

To understand what purgatory is, one needs to move from an individualistic to a community perspective. Our salvation is closely intertwined with that of others. At the moment of our death we will perhaps realize that when we failed to receive the graces that God gave us to make us saints, we also deprived other people, who are now struggling because of their sins, their pain and their suffering, whereas our holiness might have allowed the grace of God to reach them much more effectively. The soul in this situation will want of its own accord to enter purgatory through a desire of love that has nothing to do with a punishment imposed by constraint. It desires to be able to merit, that is to say, to bear fruit in love—not for itself, since it is already saved, but for others. (Purgatory is on the side of heaven; it is not a transitory antechamber of hell.)

The entire Catholic spiritual tradition prompts us to believe that the souls of purgatory, like those of paradise, are intimately associated with the salvation of men on earth and with the life of the militant church. But in heaven, all this happens without suffering, simply by intercession, because these souls are in perfect love. In purgatory, on the other hand, souls offer their suffering in love. In what does this suffering consist? First of all, they do not yet see God face-to-face. They know that they are saved and they are therefore inflamed with love for God, but they know they cannot see him because they still have to make amends for their offenses against love on behalf of those who remain in the world.

There is indeed a suffering of love that repairs the evil they have done, since sin is not only an offense to God, but also an injury to our brothers and sisters. Every sin, even the most secret, deprives others of grace in the communion of saints. Purgatory, then, is that state where, in love, souls experience something of the offering that the saints perform on earth. This is what great mystics have experienced during their lives: an extraordinary union with God, a union that is not vision but is a union of love. In purgatory this union is even much higher than that of the greatest mystics in this life.

The souls in purgatory are indeed more immediately united to God than were even the greatest saints here on earth. They are more closely united to the Lord because they have the certainty of their salvation: they have already entered irreversibly into the communion of love with God. However, they suffer from a desire of love similar to that which many mystics have known very well here below. Their suffering is caused by the fact that they do not yet see God face-to-face even though they sense intensively his presence in their hearts. At the same time, they suffer out of love because of all the misfortunes, all the distress, all the sins and sufferings that they see on earth and in which they know they have a share of responsibility. These same sins cannot cause this suffering in heaven because love superabundantly compensates everything, and because all things are seen there in the light of infinite love.

The Intercession of Souls in Purgatory

The souls in purgatory are in this sense closer to us, because they know that they themselves have been the direct or indirect cause of our sufferings, of our failings. They are happy to suffer for our sake. Reparation does not appear to them at first as an imposed punishment but as that which they desire out of love. There is a beautiful text on purgatory, which does not have a magisterial value in the Catholic Church but which is still the text of a saint: the *Treatise on Purgatory* of Saint Catherine of Genoa. Catherine, who was a mystic, insists very much on the fact that the sufferings of purgatory are quite similar to hers. All mystics tell us that they suffer tremendously because they do not yet see the God whom they long to see in the intensity of their love for him. They suffer also to see that they remain sinners and that their sins have influenced the sins of others.

To get an idea of what purgatory is like, we can also consider the inner life of Saint Francis, the sufferings of penance that he voluntarily imposed upon himself out of love, but at the same time his great joy in singing the praises of God and his creatures. Purgatory is a blessed place because it is united to heaven by the same love of God. The souls in purgatory are therefore extremely close to us. In reality, they are not any closer to us then are the saints of heaven, but we can find it easier to represent their proximity because their purification stems from a desire to repair their lack of love on earth. We inherit the consequences of their shortcomings, because these overflow onto us and onto those who come after us in this world. The souls of purgatory, in a certain sense, resemble us more. They are closely associated with us, and that is why the church asks us to pray to them and for them.

They can no longer merit for themselves, since they have reached their definitive salvation. But God asks them to pray for us and to offer us their sufferings because they have the desire to repair, as long as they have not satisfied all the love they have offended or ignored. Purgatory is a great manifestation of God's mercy. It shows that God, when he forgives us, does not simply "sponge us off," but that he respects us and takes us seriously in our acts. Only a perfect love on our part can repair our sins.

There will be no more purgatory after the resurrection of the dead. This shows that purgatory assures that our poor, suffering, sinful humanity will be accompanied by souls of the deceased until the Last Judgment and the resurrection of the dead.

The Time of Purgatory

After the final resurrection, there will be nothing but heaven and hell. Purgatory is a transitory state, related to time. Some theologians and preachers claim that all this is mythical, because as soon as one dies one is immersed in eternity, which is extra-temporal. They see no room for this intermediate time that is purgatory. According to them, the moment of our death coincides with the moment of judgment and the final resurrection.

And yet souls separated from their bodies as well, incidentally, as the angels, live in a time that is obviously not a material time like ours, measured by the hands of the clock. Their time is punctuated by events involving spiritual acts in relation to which there is a before and after. Spirits without bodies are not in the material flow of time, which for us links events together, but they grasp the events themselves in their order of succession. The angels, for example, perceive the Incarnation as an event. There was for them a before and after the Incarnation of Christ. Likewise, each of our spiritual acts is an event for our guardian angel. It is a discontinuous time, because there is no matter to assure the continuity. It is a time ordered simply by the succession of events, a purely qualitative time. In a sense it is the events themselves that take the place of hours or days in the time of purgatory.

Here let us pause in order to rectify an important misunderstanding about the time of purgatory. Some people may remember prayers for the dead where, in former times, it was stated that such and such a prayer amounted to an indulgence of a certain number of days: a "forty-day indulgence," for example. Such expressions have damaged the authentic doctrine of purgatory by inadvertently turning it into an object of derision. This expression came from a time when, during confession, penitents were asked to make amends by doing penance (on earth, of course!) for a certain number of days. These times of penance were then sometimes offered on behalf of the souls of purgatory, in the communion of saints. It was said that such and such a sacrifice, such and such a prayer or pilgrimage offered for the souls in purgatory, was equivalent to so many days of penance. It was never said that it was the equivalent of days subtracted from time in purgatory. But the distinction was subtle and many people mistakenly thought that it did refer to days in purgatory. Some people even went so far as to keep an inventory of the number of days they were subtracting from the time their departed loved ones had to spend in purgatory!

A Last Time of Grace

What is extraordinary is that God can say to a soul at the time of his death, "I still give you the grace to make amends, to offer yourself for others, now that you have really entered into my love." We probably have family members and friends who are in purgatory. We must not hesitate to pray to them and for them. Let us not forget them.

It is terrible to see how, as soon as anyone dies, he suddenly disappears from the life and worries of most people, except for those who were very close to him and for whom the period of mourning can be long, difficult, and painful. For those who are a little more removed from him in the bonds of blood and affection, the person seems to be engulfed in nothingness. The church, on the contrary, tells us, "Do not forget the souls who are in purgatory, for they do not forget you."

All those who have developed a friendship with the souls of purgatory, and are in the habit of praying for them, are unanimous in saying that they have received great graces through their intercession. It has nothing to do with a kind of bargaining; although this travesty has, alas, also existed. In reality it is an exchange of love. If we offer the souls in purgatory the love that purifies them, they give us in turn their love that suffers, and it becomes for us a source of grace.

Once again we see here the workings of the mystery of the communion of the saints that is at the very heart of Catholicism. It would seem that this aspect of the Christian faith remains obscure for our Protestant brothers and sisters. Because the Reformation lost sight of this element, it now lacks many riches relating to the sacraments and the mystery of the church. Protestantism finds it difficult to grasp the communitarian dimension of salvation, which involves a kind of interweaving of the members of the body of Christ. Protestants remained marked by the individualistic vision of the sixteenth century, where everyone was thought to have a purely vertical relationship with God in Christ. On the other hand, in the baroque paintings of the Catholic Reformation we see heaven opened in its glory, and the three levels of the church, triumphing in heaven, purifying itself in purgatory, and militant on earth.

We are all woven together in a tapestry where our lives are intertwined and, as the hero of Bernanos's *Diary of a Country Priest* declares, "There is not a kingdom of the living and another kingdom of the dead; there is only one kingdom of God, with the living and the dead, and we are all in it together."[1]

Written in the jubilee year 2000 for the remission of debts by the Lord in the Communion of Saints.

1. Translation by Casprini; the first edition of Bernanos's novel was published in 1936 by Plon of Paris, France.

www.ingramcontent.com/pod-product-compliance
Lightning Source LLC
LaVergne TN
LVHW091635100826
845152LV00002B/36

* 9 7 8 1 6 6 6 7 1 7 9 6 9 *